DATE DUE

GAYLORD   PRINTED IN U.S.A.

What Women
Voters Want
Politicians
to Hear

MELINDA
HENNEBERGER

If They
Only
Listened
to Us

SIMON & SCHUSTER

NEW YORK LONDON TORONTO SYDNEY

SIMON & SCHUSTER
Rockefeller Center
1230 Avenue of the Americas
New York, NY 10020

Designed by Karolina Harris

Manufactured in the United States of America

10   9   8   7   6   5   4   3   2   1

Library of Congress Cataloging-in-Publication Data is available.

For information about special discounts for bulk purchases,
please contact Simon & Schuster Special Sales at
1-800-456-6798 or business@simonandschuster.com.

ISBN-13: 978-0-7432-7896-6
ISBN-10:   0-7432-7896-8

For Bill, Connor, and Della

Contents

CONTENTS

If They Only Listened to Us

The Girlfriend Gap

*"What you've got to understand is
that nobody ever asks us what we think."*

I made the mistake of letting my seven-year-old twins watch President George W. Bush address the nation before we invaded Iraq, and they both burst into tears: Would Iraqi children die in the attacks? What about their moms? They were still upset—and I was still annoyed at myself—as I drove to West Virginia a few days later to meet up with my three closest friends from high school. The timing was not the best; there was snow in the forecast and "multiple terror attacks" predicted in the event of war. The threat level had just been jacked up again, so all of Washington was a little extra twitchy—and we were not a real low-key bunch to begin with.

Now that Baghdad was in shock and awe, I was tempted to stick close, with my duct tape and bottled water at the ready. But this weekend had been planned for months, in part to celebrate the end of my treatment for breast cancer, and it was a big deal for the four of us. Pam, Kim, Cathy, and I have supported each other through first dates and divorce, teen pregnancy and infertility, good fortune and loss. We've dissected every relationship in our lives and lately listened together for the disquieting

1

little scratch of mortality. In our forties, we still need to check in.

We grew up together in Mount Carmel, Illinois, population eight thousand, on a bluff overlooking the Wabash River. It's a pretty little farm town—or was, before the Target moved in, wiped out Market Street, and then moved on, like a bad storm. They all still live around there, six hours south of Chicago, in an area so conservative it went for Alan Keyes over Barack Obama for the U.S. Senate in 2004. And though I'm over a day's drive away now, we try to meet up somewhere at least once a year—sort of a *Same Time Next Year* for girlfriends—to tell secrets, swill girlie drinks, laugh at ourselves, and thank God for one another. After thirty years of friendship, I would have said we knew just about everything there was to know about one another. But I would have been wrong, because until that weekend, politics had never really come up. When it did, we found that we were as divided as the rest of the country, over the war and more.

It all started when Kim suggested that we sing patriotic songs as we hiked along, in support of the troops—and ended in a fairly astringent disagreement over whether weapons of mass destruction had been discovered in Iraq. "FOX News would have told us" if they had not been located, Kim was sure. But no such weapons had turned up yet, I insisted. She wanted to know where I got my news, and when I mentioned *The New York Times,* she laughed at what she dismissed as brand loyalty to my old employer. "You have your sources of information, and I have mine," she said.

I had just spent some time at the United Nations, working on a profile of Kofi Annan for *Newsweek,* and I had to say that nobody there seemed to think there were any WMDs to be found in Iraq; from the lowest-level functionary to the guys on the top floor, they were convinced that Iran and North Korea posed far more certain threats. But America was not about to let a bunch of wilting, Saddam-coddling diplomats tell us what was what, so telling my friends "Hey, I heard it at the UN!" was about like saying Harry Potter's house elf had come to me in a dream.

The last time any of us had quarreled like this had to have been in high school, when my friends decided I really ought to break up with my boyfriend if I had no intention of marrying him. They all did marry their teen sweethearts, the last of them at age nineteen, and had high school kids of their own by the time I made it down the aisle at thirty-three. As adults, the four of us had always respected one another's choices and taken one another's part. But now, over George W. Bush, we found ourselves taking umbrage and taking sides. Pam lined up with me, though a tad to my left; she couldn't quite bring herself to acknowledge Bush as our legitimately elected president, she said, and the other two blanched. "Are you a Democrat, Miss?" Cathy asked, calling me by my childhood nickname. There was something I had never heard before in her voice, though, and I doubted she liked it any more than I did. Was it possible that in all our hours of heavy talk, we'd never really gone there?

In Washington, political discussion is the preferred elevator music, and even children go around humming the tune. When my son, who was eight by then, learned early in 2004 that a relation of ours would be supporting neither John Kerry nor John Edwards in that year's presidential contest, he assumed this could mean only one thing, and was incredulous: "She likes *Dennis Kucinich?*" In '06, at the height of Plamegate, he burst into my room early one Saturday morning shouting, "Karl Rove has been indicted!" Then, after I snapped to consciousness: "Not really. Could you get up and make me breakfast?" My friends have alerted me to the fact that most of America does not live like this—and wouldn't want to.

We survived the contretemps, of course, and retreated to our respective bubbles. In my suburban Maryland village of aggressive recyclers, a Bush-Cheney yard sign was the talk of the town in the fall of '04, and at my polling place, John Kerry received 76 percent of the vote. Back in Mount Carmel, the smattering of "other candidates, mostly" who turned out for a campaign speech by the Democratic Party's brightest star had a hard time hearing Obama, Pam reported, over the sound of workers putting up the carnival rides for Ag Products Days. And on Election Day, 70 percent of Wabash County went for Bush. Had Kerry won the White House, I would have said that proved we'd take back the last four years if we could—that Americans do not condone torture as a tool of interrogation, or consider the Geneva Conventions even remotely "quaint." I would have said we know a mess when we see one. When he lost, however, I had nothing but questions: What did that outcome say about us? What did that result prove? For therapeutic as much as journalistic reasons, I really wanted to know.

True, I'd never met a single person thrilled beyond reason by Kerry's candidacy, including his own wife, whose underawed staff sometimes referred to him as "the husband." Yet until the very end of his timid campaign, I thought he had an even shot—because Gore did win the popular vote, and I had a hard time imagining that too many Gore supporters would look back over the last four years and conclude that Bush sure had proved them wrong.

Some did, though. Both parties improved their turnout, and "Values Voters: Myth or Must-Have" became the favorite post-election chew toy of political analysts. Another factor in Bush's win went virtually unnoticed: a small but consequential shift among women voters, who have long preferred Democrats as more reluctant to make war and more willing to fund schools and social programs. Women still favored Kerry, but the gender gap narrowed to seven points from the ten-point advantage Gore had in 2000. And in a contest this close, it mattered. As the Center for American Women and Politics at Rutgers University put it in a

post-election report, "Despite the gender gap, President Bush succeeded in increasing his overall share of the women's vote this
year . . . a major reason why he took the popular vote this time
around." A look at exactly who defected made the slippage look a
little more ominous; Kerry not only lost ground with blue-collar
women, he did worse than Gore had with the college-educated
women the party counts on. He lost support with every female demographic, in fact, except women under thirty. Black women still
voted overwhelmingly for Kerry, but the margin there also narrowed, by four points. Of the total increase in Bush's support from
women, "two thirds came from black women," says David Bositis,
a senior policy analyst at the Joint Center for Economic and Political Studies. "The shift had the most to do with moral values, and
this is something that the Republicans are using to win elections."
For those defectors, what had changed? Were American women
becoming more conservative?

We are not some monolith, of course, politically or in any
other way, and campaign season efforts to appeal to us as such—
"W. Is for Women" was surely the most overt—can seem patron-
izing. As the Democratic pollster Anna Greenberg says, with
some irritation, "We're fifty-two percent, not a minority special
interest group." Still, Kerry had made the bluntest, most
straightforward appeal—on pay equity, affordable health care,
early childhood education and a Supreme Court dedicated to up-
holding *Roe* v. *Wade*. Yet we were not sufficiently won over. Why
was that? The pat answer during the campaign was that "security moms" focusing on terror threats saw Bush as the better protector. But was that the case? What *do* women want from their
president?

After George W. Bush was returned to the White House, I
could not wait to ask them. And for answers, as usual, I turned
first to my oldest friends. As 2008 approaches, the Democrats
ought to be turning to them, too. They need to know how Kerry's

pitch on fairness in the workplace could fail to resonate with Kim, despite the long years she put in as a secretary, making male bosses look good in a company that only recently began considering women for executive positions like the one she now holds. They need to understand how Cathy, a nurse who cares for the elderly and cites health care as her number one priority, could possibly blame the Democrats for "broken promises" on that issue—even in the years they were in charge of nothing. Like Kim, she went with Bush, which made about as much sense to me as the fact that Pam and I—Catholics who voted for Kerry without a twitch or a blink—must have made to them. Clearly, I had a lot to learn.

So, soon after the '04 election, I set out just to listen—respectfully, I hoped—to women all over the country, on the major questions of our time. I wanted to hear what draws women to the Democratic Party and what sends them off screaming into the night. What were those who voted for Gore in 2000 but Bush in '04 focusing on? Were they gone for good? And if not, what would it take to get them back in '08? I didn't want to limit the discussion to "women's issues," or for that matter, to limit it at all.

I am neither a pollster nor a political strategist. I am not a polemicist with a tidy theory to prove, and did not imagine that at the finish line, I would be able to hand either party an easy six-step plan for How to Get the Girl in '08; if it were that easy, there wouldn't be so many such books. I *am* a big fan of women and their stories, though, and in listening to a couple hundred of them—234 in all, in twenty states, from Massachusetts to Arizona and Oregon to Florida—I did learn some things that both parties might like to know.

When I began, I knew only that I would start in the Midwest, where national elections are so often decided. I knew only that I would start with the women I know best, so there were a fair number of surprises along the way. But given how busy people are, one of the first and most basic was how eager women were to share their thoughts; total strangers called and cooked and then sent thank-you notes, saying they hadn't talked that much in years or felt so politically exhilarated ever. Pretty early on, I realized how starved we all are to be listened to, and how alienated from the wave upon nauseating wave of insider chitchat that is not in any real sense a national conversation. The shout culture exists in part to discourage precisely the kind of give-and-take and I-see-what-you-mean discussion that would help us work through what *we* think about and want from our government, in lieu of watching people who smile at inappropriate moments pretend to debate nonissues on cable. And wealthy or homeless, in college or retired, women said they felt disregarded by both parties. "Why would *you* want to talk to me?" they often wanted to know. Or they assumed I was hoping they would refer me to some designated "expert" or the most officially important person they knew, because that was surely who I really wanted to hear from.

While polling takes snapshots, listening takes time, and many of the interviews for this book went on for hours. They needed to, because the first thing we might blurt out about our political lives—a fragment of a campaign ad, maybe, or something our grandmother used to say—is rarely any more than a starting point. Unlike sex or religion, politics remains surprisingly private and un-examined terrain for many of us. When I began my travels, I often asked women whether their friends felt the same way they did, and frequently, the answer I got back was, "Oh, I wouldn't know; I never talk to anyone about this stuff." When they did begin to talk about it, they had blessedly few prepared answers to fall back on, but needed a minute to sort through the complicated and some-times paradoxical motivations underneath their political choices, the lifetime of impressions behind even their most "last-minute" decisions in the ballot box.

These conversations were not exactly like the journalistic interviews I'd been doing for twenty years, either, in that I tried hard not to push, prod, provoke, or even seek answers to specific questions. I have never been a big believer in the magic of clever questioning, and have long agreed with what Janet Malcolm wrote years ago in *The Journalist and the Murderer* about her discovery that people will, for their own reasons, tell their stories pretty much the same way whether in response to a brilliant question or a half-formed one. Now, I began to see that I sometimes learned the most by asking no questions at all.

I came away convinced, for one thing, that if there ever were any security moms, they must have gone into hiding in a well-stocked bunker somewhere within moments of the '04 election. All but one of the women I met who switched parties over the war on terror went the other way, abandoning Bush for Kerry. The women who found Bush a more reliable general in that war were already Republicans and would have voted for him in any case.[1]

Another surprise was how little loved Bush was even among women who had voted for him, only weeks after the election. In fact, so many women said they voted for the president *despite* mini-vanloads of misgivings, solely because they found Kerry's personality so off-putting, that I began to feel protective of the senator after a while. Was it his fault if his party didn't know better than to nominate someone who windsurfs?

Which is not to say that with no Kerry on the ticket, there will be no problem for the Democrats; on the contrary, what women

1. Even before the election in '04, Democratic pollster Anna Greenberg questioned the existence of "security moms"—a phrase coined by her fellow Democrat, the pollster Celinda Lake. In "Breaking Down the Security Mom Myth," Greenberg wrote in September of '04 that, "These 'security moms' are not a swing group, and have long been voting Republican." In the same paper, she noted that even among women who were supporting Bush, most gave reasons other than terror concerns or the war in Iraq as their major motivation for doing so. Most commonly, women said seeing Bush as a "strong leader who does what he says," was their reason for supporting him. Second was "his faith and values." Terror concerns came in third.

could not abide in Kerry was the same thing they dislike about his party. Many said they felt he in particular and Democrats in general tend to look down on middle-class Middle Americans—yes, the very people their policies are intended to lift up. How can that be? Partly, it's that "God talk" does make a lot of Democrats squirm, and that discomfort comes across to believers as condescension. As does their wholly self-destructive habit of mocking Bush and other conservatives as none too bright.

Even now, as I'm writing this in 2006, nearly two years into Kerry's *purgatorio* of coulda-shoulda-woulda, he's just suggested five ways to "get the war on terror right." Before he even got to number one, he remarked that, "Five years after 9/11, the administration still hasn't figured out how to count to five." Mild stuff, right? Harmless enough, if maybe a tad insecure? Not at all. I hope the senator is cracking himself up, because such comments alienate people who assume he and his party probably think the same of them—and how smart is that?

I expected to hear a lot from the women I interviewed about abortion, and I did, but I'm not sure the Democrats realize how many otherwise quite liberal pro-life women, Catholics in particular, have switched parties over this issue but continue to look for a way back to the Democrats, with whom they agree with on almost every other matter. These women are not just gettable, they are all but desperate to find a way home—to the point that if the party does not send a car for them, with a really respectful driver, it will have only itself to blame.

Yes, it was abortion that women who were first-time defectors from the Democrats mentioned most often. Why would that be, when *Roe* v. *Wade* was decided in 1973? Those who oppose abortion rights saw 2004 as the chance of a lifetime to overturn that decision, with a movement favorite already in the Oval Office and several spots on the Supreme Court likely to open up during the next term. A handful of Catholic bishops spoke out more plainly than in any previous election season and moved the crucial Catholic swing voters that Gore won in '00 to Bush in '04. Yet anyone who assumes such voters have found a comfy permanent home in the GOP ought to meet Kelly Dore, a former social worker and stay-at-home mom in Denver: "I'm with the Democrats on ninety percent of the issues," she says. "But if you're pro-life, they don't even want you."

I was even more taken aback, though, by the strength of opposition to gay marriage among black women; to say that the fairness argument often falls flat in the African-American community is an understatement. As Teresa Thomas-Boyd, a longtime civil rights activist in Milwaukee, puts it, "I may be discriminated against as a homosexual if I choose to say that about myself. But in a situation of color, I'm discriminated against every day. . . . When people want to make it the same, it's not, and it makes people angry."

And in discussions of the presidential race coming up in '08, I never would have expected so many women who are furious at Bush to say they see no reason to hold his party accountable for anything that has gone on during his two terms. The one question I do ask, always, of those enraged at the current administration is: "So, does that mean you're any more likely to vote Democratic in '08?" Most often, the response is not just no but "Of course not." Yes, women did come home for the '06 midterm elections, but the bags are still in the front hall, unpacked. In '06, 51 percent of all those who cast ballots were women, and 55 percent of all women voters favored a Democrat for Congress. This time, they really *were* voting over the war on terror—and against how it's being waged in Iraq. But congressional Republicans were determined in their self-destruction this year, too.[2]

---

2. In '06, California Republican Representative Randy Cunningham was sentenced to eight years in prison after admitting he accepted millions in bribes. (The haul included jewelry, French antiques, a Rolls-Royce—also used, *alors*—a $2,000 contribution to his daughter's graduation party, and free use of a yacht where he liked to entertain female guests in his jammies.)

The presidential election is different—not least because so many more women on the right than on the left seem to see it as a rolling referendum on abortion rights.

Even now, despite deep unhappiness over the war, there is still so much Democrat-on-Democrat rage out there that it's not at all unusual to hear women who have never voted for a Republican in their lives declare themselves so fed up with the home team that they are thinking seriously about Chuck Hagel—or, until he became one of the president's closest allies on Iraq, John McCain. Why? Because they've seen these men as the most effective critics Bush had, and given them extra credit for bucking their own party.

One longtime Democratic donor told me she was shocked by her own reaction to a couple of fund-raising calls she'd received. First, she heard from some poor guy from the Friends of John Kerry, to whom she responded that if he had any real friends, they would sit him down and tell him to forget about running again. Next, the Democratic National Committee rang and asked her to contribute to "help get our message out." "What message would that be?" she wanted to know. Alas, the poor kid on the phone had no idea. "But you've always given before," he begged. "And you've always wasted it!" she answered, enjoying herself a little by this

---

Former Majority Leader Tom DeLay resigned rather than risk being voted out of office; he was indicted on charges he conspired to violate campaign finance laws and tarred by his close ties to disgraced former Republican lobbyist Jack Abramoff. Abramoff went to prison this year, in one of the widest ranging influence peddling scandals in U.S. history. Two of DeLay's former aides were convicted on related charges, and Ohio Republican Representative Bob Ney resigned from office after pleading guilty to conspiracy charges, also in connection to his dealings with Abramoff.

Between Florida Congressman Mark Foley's lecherous IMs to congressional pages and Pennsylvania Congressman Don Sherwood's assertions that he so did *not* try to strangle his mistress, it suddenly became hard to argue that the Republicans owned the moral high ground. Just days before the November election, Ted Haggard, a leading evangelical minister who had gotten a share of the credit for mobilizing religious voters for Bush in '04, was accused of carrying on with a gay prostitute. By that time, it seemed that even if God were a Democrat, he was laying it on a little thick.

point. "When you find out what the message is, you can call me back, and we'll see if I like it." Until she let loose on those two unfortunates, "I hadn't even realized how angry I was" over her party's inability to provide a straightforward alternative to the disaster of the Bush years.

So many of us feel politically antagonized, for a variety of reasons, that we sometimes seem to be the new "angry white males," throwing ourselves into the scream first, ask questions later political culture with an enthusiasm I have a hard time construing as a victory for our power base. But I also wonder if much of that frustration doesn't come from feeling we need to yell to be heard at all. Increasingly, it seems, we behave as though the proper resolution of all matters facing the nation were not only obvious but OBVIOUS, so why should we ever open an ear to anything or anyone who might contradict us? We are so sure we have nothing to learn from anyone who might feel differently that we keep to our own politically—and find that the more we vent, the more we are polarized and seething.

Not long ago, a friend of mine who is an architect in L.A. told me about a trip she'd taken to Italy, where she had spent some time as a student. She had not been back to Rome in many years and was astonished when at last she did return. It was not the Eternal City that had changed. But "there was so much I didn't see before, and that I couldn't see, because I had such strong opinions about everything." We are all like that, maybe more so all the time. And I am convinced that we will never get where we need to go as a country until we can put down our shoulders for a minute and allow ourselves to be—not won over, even, but just able to hear one another again. Whatever your own politics, you will meet some women in this book with whom you agree on nothing. Yet my hope is that you will listen to them, too, and try to see why they might feel as they do.

When I first called my old pals to tell them about this completely nonlinear plan I had to get out and listen to what women were thinking about, Kim called back almost right away to say that she already had lined up more women in Fairfield, Illinois, where she lives, than I'd ever have time to talk to. "What you've got to understand," she said, "is that nobody ever asks us what we think." Upscale professional women wondering how to stay on partnership track without missing soccer practice, yes, have been heard from rather extensively. But most women in most of America, no. And that is part of the problem.

Meanwhile, in Bedford Falls

"Morally, I'm a Republican,
but environmentally, a Democrat."

There was a lot of money in Mount Carmel when I was growing up here at the tail end of the oil boom, though the truly
prosperous tended to drive pickup trucks and mow their
own front yards. Then they might indulge in the odd muffled
flourish, like formal floral arrangements for even the children's
rooms unseen by grown-ups during parties. The elegant old
homes built along bricked streets back when steamboats stopped
here on their way to New Orleans all had the same Victorian par-
lors, lined with the same uncomfortable chairs—ease being so easily overdone. And because we knew one another so well, we also
knew appearances to be highly unreliable.

It was still possible then to shop for evening wear or handmade furniture in the six-block stretch of Market Street we called
"Uptown," where there were several nice dress shops, a movie
theater, and competing jewelry stores, just steps apart, with dis-
play windows that featured dueling photo galleries of newly engaged couples, along with the china and silver patterns they'd
chosen. Twenty years ago, the first time I brought my New
Yorker husband home for the holidays, he couldn't believe how

long it took us to run a couple of errands on our bustling main street; compact as it was, we stopped so often to talk that he said he felt like he'd wandered onto the set of Bedford Falls in *It's a Wonderful Life,* with a crowd of neighbors yoo-hooing, "Merry Christmas, George!"

These days, whole minutes can go by in which nothing moves on Market Street. It's been a long time since fishermen could make a living from the river, trolling for mussel shells the Japanese used to make cultured pearls, and even the tool factory that had been a major employer since the 1930s just closed. As in so many other small American towns, Uptown has shrunk to a sad row of consignment, resale, and junk stores. Hadley's Café, where my parents first laid eyes on each other after my mother came to town to teach at the high school in 1956, is still serving the world's best coconut cream pie. But the only growth industry seems to be social services; there is a storefront Christian counseling center for pregnant girls right down the block from the county courthouse, and so little foot traffic even there that I guess no one worries that the location might be so indiscreet as to discourage business. The worn-out plastic yellow ribbons tied around the lampposts to honor the local kids serving in Iraq and Afghanistan make me want to cry, and not only for the soldiers.

Though the town overwhelmingly supported Bush in the recent election, I have not come back here to unlock the mysteries of conservative thought; for starters, even if the president's approval rating fell to 3 percent, or 0.3, those hardy few would still include my family, who when they gave me my first subscription to a periodical in the seventh grade, skipped *Highlights* and signed me up for the *Phyllis Schlafly Report.* Besides, unlike a lot of places in rural and blue-collar America, Mount Carmel has not become much more Republican over the years. This wasn't Berkeley to begin with, but almost half of Wabash County's 10,070 voters are still registered Democrats. "We're a little stronger Republican, but I don't think it matters here because people go both ways," Marie Kolb, the county clerk, tells me. "We have just a few more Republicans, but not enough to win unless you really have the people behind you." Though that's truer for local races than in presidential contests, Bill Clinton did come close in 1992, losing Wabash County by only forty-nine votes. And Bush surely had the people behind him in November 2004, when he took 70 percent of the local vote—up even from the 61 percent he got here in 2000. Was that because of the war? As it turns out, no.

Sitting in Hadley's on my first morning back in town, where I am for quite a while the only customer, I think about how the only dividing line that matters in my own small circle here—and the one that most clearly informs our politics—is the difference that was there from the start: religion. I can still see Kim at age fourteen, teary at the sight of a beer in my family's fridge, announcing that my dad was probably going to hell. Being Catholic, I heard that sort of thing pretty regularly from kids who worshipped at one of the many Bible-based Protestant churches in our town. Mount Carmel was founded by preachers, three Methodist ministers who hoped to establish a "moral, temperate, and industrious village." The civil code they drew up in 1818 criminalized swearing, drunkenness, and Sabbath breaking.

There were no minorities here when I was growing up—a legacy of the not-so-Christian "sundown laws" that forced the few blacks who worked in town but lived across the river to get out before nightfall. There were so few Jews that I never heard an anti-Semitic remark until I was grown and living in Europe. Nor were there any ethnic differences to speak of, most of us being descendants of the Germans who had settled here in several waves through the 1850s, when my great-grandfather Jacob came over from the Mosel Valley and opened a little bakery and confectionary a few miles away, just across the Indiana line. His son L.F., my grandfather, helped open a new bank in Mount Carmel, and made a go of a family business that delivered coal and ice to homes—originally, on a horse-drawn cart.

There was quite a division among the Christians in town, however, and endless arguments over such matters as whether only full-immersion baptism guarantees salvation. Though my forebears were God-fearing, too, no doubt, the strongest belief they had passed down was in the redemptive power of work. So in my summer job as a school janitor, I painted lockers and scrubbed toilets alongside a Pentecostal girl who wore ankle-length skirts in the August heat and told me I was on the fast track to the hot place because my short hair and bare legs dishonored the Lord.

My father never seemed to take reports of our likely damnation very seriously, though. Nor did he ever return fire. "That's what they believe," he'd say, and that would be it. But the drinking and dancing that went on down at the Knights of Columbus Hall definitely marked us as the town's lifestyle liberals. Politically, too, many of our fellow parishioners at St. Mary's leaned to the left in those pre–*Roe* v. *Wade* days. Because we were as far as you could get from the seat of power in the Belleville diocese, we got the priests who were going nowhere in the hierarchy, and did not, shall we say, tend to overemphasize orthodoxy. (One did run off with the mother of a schoolmate, but none were child molesters, that I ever heard, in one of the first dioceses in the country to become notorious in that regard.)[3] Our favorite pastor, Father Clyde, tooled around in a VW Bug covered with psychedelic peace signs and once waved a gun around during mass to "bring home the horrors of Vietnam."

So you could say that Pam Tenbarge and I have simply stayed

---

3. More than 10 percent of the priests in the diocese of Belleville, thirteen in all, were removed from ministry in the nineties over sex abuse allegations.

true to our anti-war, 1960s guitar-mass, post–Vatican II training at St. Mary's, just as we've remained loyal to each other since the fifth grade, when we'd call each other every night to read the latest installments of the "novels" we were always working on. Her heroines, like their creator, were blond and saucy, with adorable Bobbie Brooks outfits and chronic boyfriend troubles, while mine were determined pioneer girls who churned butter—lots and lots of butter—and tended ailing mothers. My real mother, who was in ill health much of the time, never quite approved of the friendship, the stated reason being that Pam's mom wore negligees in the middle of the afternoon.

It wasn't until our freshman year at the public high school that we got to know Cathy Fleenor and Kim Harris, who were already good friends from their own church, Parkview Christian, where punch was served at wedding receptions. We were seated alphabetically, so I sat by Kim in nearly every class and got to know Cathy through her. Later, we all ran the school newspaper together, and because we were for some reason allowed to spend two full class periods each afternoon "newsgathering," had hours a day to confer. Cath and Kim's expressed ambitions for the future centered on marriage and family, mostly, which was the norm then and there. While Pam and I had our eyes on the road out of town at all times, or so I imagined.

Periodically, I'd send off for an admissions catalog from Radcliffe—thinking, I guess, that this was where overachievers went to die—which my parents would then pitch into the trash; no way was I going anywhere in the lefty Ivy League. We were still arguing over where I might be allowed to apply when, just before Christmas in our senior year, Pam calmly announced that she was getting married in a few days, to the older brother of the boy I'd been seeing. Because she was pregnant, I was not only forbidden to attend the wedding—probably to her relief, since I could not stop sniveling—but was made to go through with a planned holiday visit to the College of William & Mary in Colonial Williamsburg, a trip I viewed as my parents' attempt to encourage my enrollment in another century.

Pam kept whatever regrets she might have had to herself; I was the one who minded the different turns our lives had taken. We never drifted apart, though, and I became godmother to her daughter, witness to her eventual annulment, and maid of honor at her wedding to the best-looking coal miner in town, who shares her political views and encouraged her to go to college in her thirties. She's a public health nurse now, working with low-income women and worrying over budget cuts that mean she can no longer offer young moms on WIC[4] a free breast pump. She has also become a professional giver of The Talk: "I've been doing puberty so long they all call me now—the junior high, the Girl Scouts. I like to do the girls; the boys are too silly." Though she freely uses her own story to encourage abstinence, "there are too many who aren't abstinent" to pretend otherwise, she says, though that is what she is supposed to do. "I have to be careful."

That first night I'm back in town, on our way to pick up Pam's husband, Stan, for their daughter Chloe's high school basketball game, we pass the old Snap-on Tools factory, which opened here in 1937. After working nights and weekends to earn a college degree in his thirties, too, Stan had finally been able to quit the mine and get a business-side job at Snap-on, a job he loved until the day the place was shuttered. "Stan was still working there last year this time," Pam says as we pass the empty building, which has a for-sale sign out front.

Stan is waiting for us in the parking lot outside the mine, so exhausted he's even quieter than usual. There have been four roof-

4. WIC is the Special Supplemental Nutrition Program for Women, Infants, and Children. It provides food, nutrition counseling, and access to health care for low-income women, infants, and children up to age five.

falls in the seven months since he went back to work there, and he takes his new job overseeing safety very seriously, constantly walking the mine to the point that he's having trouble keeping weight on. Though he's discouraged on the job front, "the one thing I can do for him now is feed him," Pam says softly, "so I'm trying to do that really well."

At the game, we say hi to our old geometry teacher and sit down with Pam's mom, Sharon—still glamorous as ever in her sixties—who says that for the first time in her life, she didn't bother voting in '04, mostly because she found the idea of the new electronic voting machines too intimidating. Had she cast a ballot, she says, she would without question have gone for Kerry, though she's been back and forth between the political parties in past races. "I didn't really pay much attention until the debates, but I thought Kerry just mopped the floor with Bush. But no one else saw that, I guess. Then people criticized his wife and said she was not nice, but I thought she was great. Some of my friends raved about Bush, so I tried not to say anything. But one said, 'I couldn't vote for Kerry because of my religion.' And she's *Catholic*! I thought, 'Oh, how small-minded.' I don't like Bush's whole body language. You can tell a lot about a person from their body language, and he's such a cocky little thing." So, why didn't she vote for the other guy? "Isn't that awful?" she says.

I hear a lot of that kind of talk from women here, and a lot of sentences that begin and end with disclaimers: "Of course, this is only me talking, and I could be wrong." Sharon's granddaughter Chloe is the high scorer in the game, and she's a good student, too, so Pam and Stan are naturally thinking about college scholarships. Chloe, meanwhile, is thinking about West Point, at the urging of a local alum. "I swear this child is not from me," Pam tells me during the game. "I am not helping her" get an appointment to a military academy, "and I don't know if that's why she's so gung ho. She's got friends who are going to Iraq. She's a good kid, so maybe this is her form of rebellion. I keep saying, 'For Christ's sake, Chloe, there's a war on!' But I'm afraid of talking it down too much."

Next morning, a weekday, I head to early mass at St. Mary's, where there are five people in attendance and I know three of them. They've just finished a beautifully done restoration of the old church, where I used to hide at recess, preferring pleasant chats with the Virgin Mary to embarrassing myself at softball. But the weekly parish bulletin tells me the place hasn't changed so much; under the heading of KUDOS, there is a shout-out to those who helped celebrate Catholic School Week and another to those who brought cans of soup for the hungry on "Soup-er Bowl Sunday." Then this item: "Kudos to the National Organization of Bishops and Priests of Australia for being the first national group to encourage optional celibacy to help the priest shortage."

The pastor, Father Bill Rowe, a former air force chaplain, is known for the brevity of his homilies, including the one in which he derided *The Passion of the Christ* as "the Gospel according to Mel." After mass, he sits down with me at a table in the new meet-and-greet space and observes that the majority of his fifteen hundred parishioners do seem to favor the Republican Party these days—chiefly over abortion, "though there are a lot of poor people in the area, and they'd be the first to reach out to help someone in trouble. We have a sister parish in Guatemala. And they haven't thrown me out yet."

Nor did his flock "buy that whole thing of refusing communion" to pro-choice politicians. "When we have weddings or funerals, I say everybody is welcome to receive, and I've brainwashed them enough that even the older people say, 'Boy, I'm glad we do that now.' Most of our parishes in southern Illinois are more liberal or open, so I just wonder what will happen when the younger priests come in trained under this pope." John Paul II, he means.

"People here still talk about how Clyde"—he of the psychedelic VW Bug—"challenged them to see church as worldwide and caring for the poor as our first job as Christians."

Not all of my fellow Catholics at St. Mary's have gone over to the GOP, of course, and some are reverse security moms who switched to Kerry over the war. After Father Bill goes off to fix something in the church, I stop in across the street at the Catholic Charities office to see Cindy Crumley, who is in my photo album wearing red velvet on our double date to the homecoming dance freshman year. Cindy married a guy a couple of years ahead of us who does construction and roadwork in season, while she does casework here and cleans the church for extra cash. The youngest of their five kids made the news the previous summer for catching Ken Griffey, Jr.'s five hundredth home-run ball at a game in St. Louis. "We could have paid for his college with what that ball would have brought, but he gave it back to Ken Griffey," she says, proud that he'd resisted the temptation to cash in. "People thought he was crazy."

Cindy used to vote Republican and got a lot of pressure to go with Bush this time: "My mom said I couldn't vote for Kerry because he's for abortions, but she knows nothing about the man except he's a baby killer." In the end, Cindy took her twenty-four-year-old marine son's advice instead. "He's in Iraq, and he said, 'Mom, you can't vote for Bush because he wants to keep us over here.' Jared gets out in May, and it's been a long four years."

But over lunch at Hadley's with Pam and me, another former classmate, Jeanne Condol, reports that her son was one of only two kids in the eighth grade at St. Mary's to cast a vote for Kerry in their mock election. "And the other kid was French! They just moved here. Clay told his class he didn't like Bush because of Iraq, and Johnny Trimble said, 'Yeah, but what about abortion?' They put some pressure on him, but he stayed with Kerry. Just him and Adrien." Jeanne, who is a CPA, is agitated still about the election, though she hadn't been much of a partisan in the past. "I'm an independent; I didn't vote for Clinton either time. And even though I did vote for Gore, it was only when we went into Iraq that I really lost it" for Bush. "He's made us less safe and created thousands of new terrorists who would think nothing of killing Americans, including my kids." "I just want a president who doesn't make stupid faces," Pam puts in, and an older man walking by our booth turns around and gapes at her.

Though Jeanne's dad was a prominent local Democrat, her mom, Viola Kieffer, has turned Republican in recent years, and after our meal, we drive out to see her. Sitting in Vi's kitchen brings back memories of Paleolithic slumber parties with a Carole King soundtrack. The print of van Gogh's *The Potato Eaters* that used to hang on the far wall has been retired, I notice, and there are likenesses of Jesus and George Bush propped up around the room now. "We don't any of us like this war; he opened up a big can of worms when he went there," Vi says. But, no surprise, "abortion is my main reason" for switching parties. "A lot of my kids"—Jeanne is the youngest of six—"didn't like the way I voted, but I did it anyway."

In fact, almost every woman I talk to here mentions abortion as part of her Election Day calculus. And that includes every one of my friend Cathy's coworkers at an agency that provides in-home nursing care in Evansville, Indiana, forty miles away. Those who mention the war at all do so to explain why they voted for Kerry. "This is the only time in my life I voted Democrat, but the war was huge," says one of them, Kim Licht, who works in medical records. "My dad was in World War Two, and he thinks this war is horrible. He says not one boy will come back normal, and I just think it was unjustified. I'm still feeling a little guilty over my vote because of abortion, but what cushions me on that is that there was a little back-alley doctor who some of my friends went to for abortions for fifty dollars, and they would bleed for weeks."

Even I am slightly startled by how open to Democratic persuasion these women are; as white married women in supposedly deep-red Indiana, they are a demographic considered increasingly out of reach for the blue team in a state the party had long written off. Yet to hear them tell it, their problem with the Democrats is pretty singular: It begins and ends with abortion.[5] Yvonne Hardy, a nurse and homesteader who grows all of her own food, sums up the tension this way: "Every time I vote, it makes me sick. Because morally, I'm a Republican, but environmentally, a Democrat." In the end, she usually votes what she thinks of as her morality over her pocketbook, and her planet.

Income inequality in this country is not widely seen as a moral issue, though the middle class is not just losing ground— it's disappearing. In the Bush years, the already advantaged have been pampered to the point that the distribution of both wealth and income is now more unequal that at any time since the Great Depression.[6] So why are tax cuts that heavily favor those least in need *not* a moral issue? Why is a dignified retirement for working

---

5. These women explain a lot about why Indiana turned blue the next year, in '06. With social issues taking a backseat to mounting concerns over the war, voters in the eighth congressional district, which includes Evansville, had quite a turnaround, and Democratic challenger Brad Ellsworth easily beat Republican incumbent John Hostettler, taking 61 percent of the vote to the incumbent's 39 percent. Elsewhere in the state, two other Republican incumbents were voted out in key races—Chris Chocola lost to Joe Donnelly in the second congressional district, and Mike Sodrel to Baron Hill in the ninth. Democrats also took control of the Indiana House.

6. Before the Democrats took control of Congress, the federal minimum wage had not gone up since 1997, and when adjusted for inflation was worth less than at any time in the last fifty years. Real wages in manufacturing fell 1 percent between 1980 and 2004, while the real income of the richest 1 percent rose 135 percent. In the Bush years, the disparity has widened rapidly; according to the nonpartisan Economic Policy Institute, the percentage of wealth held by the richest 1 percent shot up from 173 times that of the average household in 2001 to 190 times that of the average household by 2004. There were seven million more uninsured Americans by 2005 than when Bush was elected in 2000.

people not a moral imperative? How do Republicans get away with policies that benefit so few?

The answer that comes through here is unambiguous: Americans prefer to think of themselves as voting for something more than their own economic interest. And while Republicans routinely offer a claim on the moral high ground—a vote for life!—that's ground the Democrats have barely set foot on since Bill Clinton turned us into a party of pragmatists, though he talked about God easily enough. Even with Clinton's superior skills, and the gift that Ross Perot's third-party candidacy turned out to be, it was as a "different kind of Democrat," willing to shred the safety net, that he broke the Republican lock on the presidency. It would be hard to argue that the country didn't benefit as a result, but Clinton's party did lose something in the bargain: our sense of ourselves as Democrats. And without that, no amount of Republican bungling will assure a win by default.

Wake up and smell the incense, people. This is a country of true believers, and yet here we are, so ashamed to show any embarrassing trace of bleeding-heart idealism that we're happy to let the party of big business play the misty-eyed romantics. There are so many voters like Yvonne Hardy who are struggling to do the moral thing at election time. Yet our answer, condescending as well as off-point, is to assume that education is all that's lacking— "Would somebody get this woman a calculator?"—and to talk all the louder about what's in it for her. So if Yvonne thinks voting her values means opposing abortion rights, period, whose fault is that?

Other than abortion, the rationale I hear cited most often by Democratic defectors is the perception that Kerry and his party are elitists who condescend to Middle Americans, to believers in general and Christians in particular. One woman who feels this way is another former classmate, Carol Woodard, whose farm family raised corn, soybeans, and Democrats. Carol was always way out of my league, coolness-wise—a funny, funky hippie chick who partied, sang in a band sometimes, and hung out with gay guys. Who might not be quite what you have in mind, in other words, when you think "values voter." Yet Carol, who's a cardio-rehab nurse and single mom, sums up why she voted Republican in '04 this way: "I just felt like we were being discriminated against"—the "we" in this case being Christians. Though I don't agree, I don't think this came to Carol in a FOX-fomented dream, either. So many midwesterners say they hear cultural condescension coming at them from national Democrats that it would be a mistake to write off this notion as mere spin. And women, who so often are underestimated, seem particularly alive to these perceived slights.

Though the president's family may be more Kennebunkport than Crawford, the first President Bush knew what he was doing when he took up with Lee Greenwood and the Gatlin Brothers— and probably laughed harder than anyone when he heard about Whoopi Goldberg's blue Bush jokes at a Kerry fund-raiser during the '04 campaign. (You know, the funnies that W.'s campaign manager said showed Kerry "doesn't share the same values" as the rest of America, delighted to suggest yet again that Democrats relate a lot more to the coasts, to Hollywood and Harvard, than to Mr. and Mrs. Normal living anywhere in between.) During the same gala, at Radio City Music Hall, comedian Chevy Chase joked about the president's supposedly feeble intellect: "This guy's as bright as an egg timer." It's this kind of casual, highly expendable slam on Bush's brainpower that offends Middle Americans more than Whoopi's dirty jokes. Conservative pundits live for such comments. For decades, they've been using them to convince average Americans of liberal snootiness—by exploiting our insecurities and making us wonder, *"Do* I resemble that remark?" But knowing that's the case makes the fact that Democrats carry right on making such cracks, which are not even irresistibly hilarious, all the more puzzling—and, though I never like my children to use this word, not a little stupid.

In the teachers' lounge at the public high school in Fairfield, Illinois, where Kim's husband, Dana, teaches math, I hear multiple variations on this theme of condescension. "Look," says Pam Robbins, "I used to be a Democrat, and I'm still very much Independent. I voted for Clinton. I'm religious but not a fanatic; I see a lot of gray. My mother has Alzheimer's, so I'm for stem cell research, and I'm not against people's right to an abortion." But Kerry "just struck me as arrogant," she says, while Bush gave her "the feeling that this was a more open person who would not be, 'I'm important and you're not.'" Another teacher at the table, Lori Robson, gets a huge laugh when she says, "Kerry just did not rub me right. His whole demeanor—I felt like he thought he was better than us. Even though Bush is from a wealthy family, *he* doesn't look down on us."

There is no point in arguing, is there? In politics, the difference between perception and reality could hardly be more meaningless. The tepid-to-turned-off response to Kerry is all the more damning to those who chose him, given how few Bush voters— even in counties that went for him 70–30—offer anything approaching a wholehearted endorsement of the man just a few months after the election. And for the Democrats, the scary thing is not that Kerry was the wrong candidate, but that they couldn't see that walking away.

Surely one of the president's most convinced critics here is Pam's boss at the Wabash County Health Department, Patti Skees, who motions me into her office at the old railroad depot. "Well, I'm not pro-choice," she starts in, "but I'm not going to stop abortion by legislating it; I'm going to stop it by supporting family planning. And you can bet if Jenna or Barbara got knocked up—" She stops herself. "Some people think Bush has got the red phone right to God, and that terrifies me. He's just a money boy, an oil-money boy, is all, and if you look into his background, you will see he is not an ethical man." Patti's husband, a salesman, "sees the economy getting better. Of course, he's not buying the groceries, mind you, and I don't see that. But this inauguration, and the money they spent on that when we're at war really torqued me off. I thought, 'Take one of those designer dresses off one of those twins and armor us a tank.'"

Most others in the health department seem to disagree, though they see the results of Republican social policy every day: "I'm a registered Democrat, and I'm *not* for being in Iraq, but I'll tell you what, I voted for Bush," offers one of Pam's colleagues, Candy Kemper. "I don't know that Bush is totally truthful, and he's not the smartest person in the world, but Kerry, I really didn't like his wife, and that influenced me. She has a smart mouth and doesn't control it." Another voter put off by the smarty-pants party. It is not, as you often hear frustrated Democrats say, that average voters don't want a smart president; they just don't want a president who comes across like he thinks the rest of us are none too bright.

Though it's no comfort, I do think that perception is partly a matter of miscommunication across a regional divide. How would I know? Because after two decades with my husband, I am able still to confound him with the odd down-home expression, and it's a matter of tone even more than of words; there are still times he thinks I'm shooting for irony when, no, I'm perfectly sincere. The very last time I uttered the phrase "You are too kind!"—to a *New York Times* colleague who had just handed me a Christmas present— she was so sure I was being sarcastic that she nearly took it back. Yet I am nevertheless forced into service as some kind of hobbled cultural mediator, defending my fellow midwesterners to my father-in-law, who regularly voices his feeling that not a lot of brain strain goes on out there in America. Then I defend my fellow East Coast liberals to my father, who finds us a generally insufferable lot of dissolute know-it-alls. One of my own pet peeves in this regional standoff is the notion that midwesterners are all mounds of flesh whose favorite treat is Cheez Whiz on white bread, with maybe a Mountain Dew chaser, topped off by some HoHos. So I had to laugh when Kim and Pam came to visit me last year and one of Kim's first observations on Washington was "Where are all the fat people?"

Mount Carmel is in all ways closer to Nashville than Chicago, an hour's drive from the Kentucky line. Early in my marriage, my father-in-law used to pretend he had trouble penetrating my slightly southern-tinged accent. "What did she say?" he'd ask my husband. The first Thanksgiving we were married, we invited both families to our apartment in Manhattan. Making conversation over the traditional yams smothered in marshmallows, my mother told a story about accompanying me to the English as a Second Language (ESL) class I taught at our church in Chelsea. My father-in-law exploded in laughter: "Imagine the poor immigrants walking around New York with an accent like Melinda's!" I can still see the WMD-level look my mother shot him that Thanksgiving, and probably, so can he. So it's telling, I think, that my continuing to get together with my oldest friends puzzles even her: "You have nothing in common with them anymore." Though she, too, objects to what she sees as the condescension of the East Coast intelligentsia, even she wonders what we have to talk about.

The last night I am in town is "girls' night in" and Cath, Pam, and I meet at Kim's, where we are in no time sprawled out over every piece of furniture in her living room, sipping wine and mainlining munchies. Kim picks up right where we left off on the hiking trail in West Virginia: "You were right that the WMDs have not been found. But it's so difficult for me to second-guess a whole government and think they just sent kids to war for fun." Not for fun, no, I say, eager to agree. "Honestly, I'm just not that political," she says, and for a minute, there is comity tonight. But then Pam remarks, "It's a shame Clinton got raked over the coals, when FDR had a girlfriend, too, and JFK . . ." Five minutes later, we are not only talking, and all at once, but shouting, and then laughing, about Bill and Hill. "Weren't we having this discussion about Bush?" Kim says. "What *is* it about the Clintons?"

Whatever it is, it is stronger than we are. "I think Bush is as much an old coot as any of the rest of them, and has probably pulled some deals in his time," Kim continues, "but Bill Clinton was so disrespectful to his little—He had a *daughter.* I mean, for four to eight years, behave your frigging self!" For her, it's the lack of respect that rankles as much as the bad-boy behavior. When another moratorium on Clinton talk is called, Cath at first says her central complaint is that the Democrats "have too many broken promises" on health care. I ask if she means the health care legislation the Republican Congress blocked back when Clinton was president, and Kim asks if I'm here to argue or learn something; point taken. But as we keep talking, Cath makes clear that it's not really health care that's driving her politics: Her father, a union welder who died too young, had always said that the GOP was better for business—a business like the construction company Cathy's brother and husband are partners in, for instance, which is doing well enough that they have been able to buy a lake house. Well enough that she can at least aspire to a big tax break.

Pam can't quite let that go by: "Oh, really? Ask Jerry Tenbarge"—her dad, who was a Pepsi-Cola distributor. "He was always a Republican, too, until his small business got bought out from under him," after Pepsi did away with their middlemen. Cath regrets having touched a nerve, and says, "Those corporations are too rich to even fathom what middle-class people go through."

But that in turn sets Kim off. "You say middle class, and I'm not even middle class! I work sixty hours a week, and Dana works full-time plus three classes a week at night, and that's just my life." She wants to know what bugs me so much about the current administration, anyway, and when I mention the environment, among other things, she says she finds that funny. "We're already regulated to death," Kim says, "and if they don't ease up on all those environmental regulations, we won't have any more manufacturing in this country. So if you're telling me he's eased it at all, you're making me like him more." As a mom, doesn't she worry that we're poisoning the planet? Not at all, she says. "But I guess it just goes back to the whole religious thing again. I put my faith in God. I don't think we're poisoning the planet, but even if we are, then maybe that's how this planet is supposed to end." And though I don't gasp at that or anything, I do have to concede in my own mind that there are some fissures even friendship cannot backfill.

More concrete and urgent to Kim than any danger posed by dying coral reefs is her everyday reality as a components buyer at Airtex, an automotive fuel and water-pump maker headquartered here and recently sold to the Carlyle Group. She's doing a job that she says would have kept several people employed full-time a decade ago. "I buy thirty million dollars a year in inventory from all over the world, and have to make sure we get the components on time, but not too soon so we're not holding inventory," she explains. "If a ship breaks down and we don't get a plastic cap we need, we have to send people home, so sometimes you're flying stuff in from Germany or China and spending twelve hundred dollars to ship in three hundred dollars' worth of product, and then you have to explain to upper management why you had to do that." Since the new management came in, "now it's accountability, and it's cut, cut, cut. Maybe I'm wrong," she says pointedly, "but I don't remember you ever working for a place like that."

Working, in other words, in a contracting—some would say

dying—industry like ink-on-paper journalism, for instance? Thousands of American journalists lost their jobs in the last year alone, I tell her, hurt that she wouldn't see the common ground. "It's not the same," she argues. "You have a choice." The choice she is referring to—to work for pay or not—is a loaded word in this context, too. But the demographic differences she's flicking at, of education and income, are not nearly as insignificant as I have always *chosen* to think. Despite deep affection, there is a dishearteningly wide cultural divide even here in Kim's living room. And for the moment at least, I am stuck in the John Kerry role.

The Gator That Got Away (with Your Ballot, Hillary's Hopes, and Katherine Harris's Little Blue Suit)

"Every day that I wake up and we're not under martial law is a good day."

It has come to this: I actually feel sorry for Katherine Harris. My husband, who as anyone will tell you is one accepting guy, says that this time I am on my own. But then, he is not with me in Florida, where two stories are dominating the news this week, dwarfing even the latest first-person accounts of what it feels like to pay three dollars a gallon for gasoline. The first of these tales involves the three women, in three different parts of the state, who have been killed in alligator attacks in the last ten days. Scientists figure it's the drought—Global Warming Alert #439, for those of you keeping tabs—that has sent these prehistoric cousins of the dinosaurs crawling through suburbia in search of sustenance, hungrier than usual and more aggressive, in the middle of mating season. A fourth woman was nibbled on the ankle while gardening, but punched her attacker in the snout and lived to watch him saunter away. So, pretty much everyone is walking around with his head down and at least one eye peeled for dehydrated gators. Apparently, we are as adaptable as they are; we learn to compensate, then not to notice. One woman I meet here, from Deltona, tells me she barely even looks up now when she walks past the smallish one that has moved into the fountain outside the Seminole County sheriff's office where she does clerical work, though it can still get dicey when he crawls under a parked car for a nap. I for one am carrying around an umbrella, not in case of rain but for snout-punching purposes, should the need arise.

The story that's even more talked about here this week is the one about how Katherine Harris wore the wrong thing to meet the president and his brother, the governor, when they visited here the other day. I don't mean wrong as in oops, dressy casual to the cookout where everyone else was in jeans, either. No, as strategic and stylistic errors go, you had to admire the boldness of the thing. For her meeting on a steamy tarmac with the Bush boys, right after Jeb Bush informed the world that Harris had no hope of winning her Senate race, the congresswoman refused to retreat into anything remotely resembling the navy suit that taste, decorum, and every consultant in the multiverse would have dictated. Instead, she went with a getup that a fashion writer for *The Tampa Tribune* described as "a body-hugging, sea foam green suit with lace trim, slit skirt, green open-toed slingback shoes and a multi-strand pearl choker." She looked alluring, definitely, like she was ready for her close-up on Italian television. But, though I don't like to be vulgar, the whole thing was screaming "*!#@ me" so loud it kind of came out like "And you, and the horse you rode in on—even if, in case you've forgotten, that would be me!" Ill-advised as this sartorial tirade obviously was, the one thing it did not seem was unintentional. All the political and fashion commentators said she was off-message that morning, looking so unsenatorial, but I don't see how she could have been any clearer; this was one angry sister. You can spurn me, her ensemble said, but ignoring me is not an option. Who says there's no personality left in politics?

I have come here, to the I-4 corridor that cuts across central Florida, where swing voting is a way of life, to meet some of the uncertain souls without whom the hanging chads would not have mattered and the W. years would not have happened. On the flight down, I imagined myself cruising from Daytona to Tampa, randomly accosting Floridians and beseeching them to tell me: Why? Why? But I'm barely settled into my "resort" accommodations behind the T.G.I. Friday's in Kissimmee, outside Orlando—on what's surely the longest stretch of road in America without a Starbucks—before I begin to see that this is not the right question. What we most need to know is not so much the why as the how—as in, how can those of us who believe that every vote counts be sure that our votes are counted? The 2002 Help America Vote Act was supposed to restore voter confidence with electronic voting technology, but widespread problems with the new machines have had the opposite effect.[7] And just about every woman I talk to here convinces me that without serious election reform, nothing else the Democrats do will matter.

My first stop is to see Thalia Potter, matriarch of one of Tampa's oldest neighborhoods, Seminole Heights, in the house she and her husband built fifty years ago on the Hillsborough River. By the oversize standards of today's waterside McMansions, it is a cottage, shaded by palm trees and ringed with hibiscus, with a deck right on the lip of the river she stays busy trying to protect from polluters, EPA officials (who these days favor a looser, not so Clean Water Act), and condo developers, like the ones trying to

7. In Katherine Harris's old congressional district in Sarasota, for example, electronic voting machines reported that Republican Vern Buchanan beat Democrat Christine Jennings in a squeaker—by only 369 votes out of 238,000 votes cast. But the machines also reported that some 18,000 of the Sarasota County voters who showed up at the polls that day—15 percent of them—did not cast a ballot in the congressional race. Which is especially difficult to believe because in all the counties in the 13th district that use optical scan machines, the undervote ranged from 2.2 to 5.3 percent. And if the undervote was actually somewhere more in line with the 2.5 percent of absentee voters in Sarasota County, then thousands of votes were not counted. State officials have nonetheless certified Buchanan as the winner, and Jennings has gone to court to petition for a new election. The new Congress has seated Buchanan provisionally, pending its own investigation.

buy out the little shipyard adjacent to her property, which has been in operation since before the Civil War. Thalia hasn't seen any gators lately but is relieved that the city has finally posted signs in Epps Park next to her house, warning people against letting their dogs run and swim free there. Alligators "love dogs," she says. "They're attracted to the aroma."

Though no fan of Katherine Harris, Thalia has had the congresswoman on her mind in recent days. "Do you suppose they would have treated a man like that, if he had done for them what she did?" she asks, referring to Harris's dual role in the 2000 election, when she served as both Florida's secretary of state, responsible for certifying the election results, and as the Florida chairwoman of Bush's presidential campaign. "I realize it's partly because she's so mixed up and unhinged, but I really believe any man in politics who had done what she did for the Republican Party would have demanded and gotten more recognition."

(The completely unsubstantiated talk in Florida is that Harris had been promised a pearl of an ambassadorial appointment, after five years finally gave the president a deadline, threatening that she would run for the U.S. Senate if it was not met, and is now making good on that threat, as a kind of political suicide bomber.[8] Harris has been denying she ever sought such a promise as far back as the recount itself, when *Saturday Night Live*'s Ana Gasteyer played her, burbling that she had no intention of settling for a posting in "some sad country where everyone is poor and sick all the time. I'm going to a good country, where they have nice clothes and speak English.")

Even if she never becomes Madam Ambassador, Harris has already gone down in history in my neighborhood. Last summer, a

---

8. If that was the case, it was mission accomplished: Harris lost to Democrat Bill Nelson in a lopsided race in which she took just 38 percent of the vote to his 60 percent, according to the Florida Department of State.

bunch of couples got together for a progressive dinner. Given the demographics of our village, some people assumed that meant it was a Democratic fund-raiser, but no. When my husband and I joined the others for dessert, they were playing a game, taking turns pulling questions out of a bag. One was: "If you could go back for a do-over of one moment in history, what moment would it be?" That turned out to be kind of a dud discussion-wise, though, because as soon as we decided to exclude the holocaust and all genocide, there was quick consensus that the 2000 presidential election was the weed we'd most like to tug. (I considered arguing that the Fall of Man was pretty bad, but you have to be in just the right mood to take things in that direction.)

Now, Thalia is a strong Democrat and longtime environmentalist who started her own file on global warming in the 1980s. "When Greenland disappears," she drawls, "even the Republicans will have to recognize it." She was a public servant herself for twenty-two years, starting out as a secretary to a "good-old-boy sheriff" of Hillsborough County and winding up her career as an aide to Congressman Jim Davis—who is running for governor this year[9]—when he was in the Florida legislature. But "then it was only politics at election time," she notes, patting her waves of short white hair. "The rest of the time, it was *government*."

She worked hard for Al Gore, but a little less so for John Kerry, and is not planning to pull out the stops in '08. "I've just had so many disappointments; I'm tired of working in campaigns and having it not pan out." It's not so much the losing, she says, as it is the not knowing whether her candidate really lost. "I'm not sure the last two elections have been won" by the Republicans, she says, lowering her voice, though it is only the two of us in her living room, along with her cat, who is curled up next to her on the

9. Davis lost to Republican Charlie Crist, 45 to 51 percent.

couch. And naturally, this erosion of faith in the integrity of the process has taken its toll.

Thalia seems quite a careful person, quick to laugh but not to disparage, as so many of us do, on the basis of presentation. She takes her own notes on our conversation and declares herself taken aback by the ferocity of her own opposition to the current administration. Yet for some time, she has been wondering if her party realizes what it is up against, or is working as intently as it might be to make future elections unstealable: If the Democrats didn't really lose, then the only lesson to be learned from the last two presidential races is that the need for election reform could hardly be more urgent. Thalia's only significant unhappiness with her party is that they seem not to grasp this fully. "They have a naïveté" even now, she feels, that if they work harder and smarter, everything will come out all right.

In Washington, any mention of stolen elections or "fixed" electronic voting machines is considered more than a little crackpot, roughly on a par with announcing that if you play the theme from *Law and Order* backward, you can hear Nostradamus predicting 9/11. Given the long and well-established history of voter fraud in this country, I fail to see why either party should be considered above attempting to improve upon the election results— buff them up a little, for the good of the people. But for argument's sake, let's say it is pure fantasy to imagine that Diebold, the leading manufacturer of automated election machines, whose former top executive was also a Bush fund-raiser, would leave the system vulnerable to manipulation. Let's drop the whole notion that Katherine Harris was anything other than neutral in the way she tidied up the registration rolls in Florida in 2000, and imagine that Ohio's '04 voter lists were purged in a similarly unbiased fashion by that state's Republican secretary of state, Ken Blackwell. Let's call it luck of the draw that mostly white, Republican suburbs in Ohio were allocated plenty of voting machines in '04, while in mostly black, Democratic urban areas, there were so few that some people ended up waiting in line in the rain for twelve hours. Still, *still,* when the system has become so suspect that a lifelong committed voter like Thalia Potter has lost heart, how is that not a problem?

Though she does believe that Al Gore was elected the first time, Thalia is not among those hoping he will run again. She tells about a gathering she attended here in the early stages of the 2000 campaign, where the vice president met with a group of local supporters. "We gathered and we waited and we waited, and we forgave him for that." But after the meeting, "he left that room without shaking one hand. I remembered reading Carl Jung about introverts—Jung was an introvert, too—and he said that when an extrovert goes to a party, he's thinking, 'I wonder who will be there?' and the introvert is thinking, 'I wonder what will be expected of me?' And I could see that pattern with him, that every time there was an opportunity not to do something," like shake a hand, "he didn't do it, so that there was not that devotion" from supporters.

The other time she was in the room with Gore was at four A.M. on Election Day, the last stop of his presidential campaign, only hours before the polls were to open. "And I have yet to shake his hand." Which was not so much a disappointment, she says, as it was a window—possibly even into why he gave up the post-election fight without ever demanding a full recount. She sighs at all the country lost as a result: "I thought we were going to have a president I would respect."

Republicans here also tend to mention the uncertainty surrounding the last two elections, if only to bat down the suspicions. Denise Kent, for instance, who fixes Thalia's hair and has twin sons who will be high school seniors next year, begins, "I went for Bush and didn't have any issues with it, but my husband feels differently; he thinks it was probably rigged. I don't like to think that." None of us likes to think we made a mistake in choosing our candidate. But when she puts it that way—"I don't like to think that"—it echoes a passage in the book I'm reading, *Truth & Beauty: A Friendship* by Ann Patchett: "I knew I had made a mistake almost as soon as I moved in with Dennis," she writes of the man she later married and divorced, "and now I had to find a way to fix that mistake without the embarrassment of breaking up with him and moving again. In short, I had to make it work." Maybe it's not the president's decisions we are so invested in defending, but our own.

When asked how she feels about Bush now, Denise says she no longer approves of the war and has some problems with the president's advisers. "I'm *fairly* happy," she says, but in a tone that, were she using it to describe her marriage, would make me think she already had the lawyer's number in her purse. "They should stop the war, that would be the biggest thing. He's made some bad choices on who works underneath him, and they've made him look bad." For now, at least, she is still trying to make it work.

That night I meet Jeannie Economos, an organizer for the Farmworker Association of Florida, at a little Greek restaurant in her neighborhood in Orlando. When I drive past the place, looking for parking, I have her figured for the woman on the patio with the flowing salt-and-pepper hair, wearing glasses and a wide-open "I don't know the person I'm meeting" expression. No doubt she easily spots me, too, in my white rental car and a black dress that makes me feel like a Tom Wolfe wannabe—so obviously not from around here, in the land of floral prints, that when I was lost earlier and pulled up in front of a pawnshop the size of a Kmart, a salesguy doing business in the parking lot took one glance and said, "Directions?"

Jeannie and I take a table outside, where there is a nice little breeze coming off Lake Ivanhoe across the way. Before they can bring on the melitzanosalata, Jeannie has a confession: "This is going to be disturbing. But I did vote for Nader in 2000." Oh? (With advanced interviewing techniques like this, I might as well have been a psychotherapist.) "I thought it would be a chance to get a third party" energized, she explains. She can't say she regrets it, either, because she was following her conscience. "I was torn" right up until Election Day. "But then a friend who is a Green said, 'At some point, we have to stand up for a third party.' If the Democrats were doing the right thing, they would have the voters." Which was Nader's justification all along, his rationalization for making his candidacy work.

Anyway, "I really do think we didn't lose," either in 2000 or in 2004. "And I'm afraid about this next election." Jeannie can pinpoint the moment she came into her own politically, as a sophomore at Furman University in Greenville, South Carolina: "We had gone to a philosophy professor's house, and we were talking about the morality of abortion—not the reality of women's lives—and on the way home, we drove past some homeless people, and someone said, 'Oh, the *gray* people.' So I quit, hitchhiked, and went out to be with the *gray* people. I didn't want to be coddled; I worked in factories, saw bad things, got mugged, and did that for thirteen years. Then my mom got sick." She moved home and cared for her mother, who, she says, "would have liked for me to finish college and have a family and a home, but she also respected me. I could say everything to her. Mother's Day is the hardest day of the year for me."

Though Jeannie grew up here and has been back for years, she has never gotten used to living in such close proximity to Mickey and Dumbo, not to mention Princess Jasmine: "When I see Epcot, I see what used to be—orange groves and forests. We used to spray-paint 'You're destroying the homes of raccoons!' over there." She laughs ruefully. "Those little actions seem *so* little now, and environmental work is so painful. You tear down trees and put in concrete, and it only makes it hotter." She finds the whole Disneyfied town of Celebration "just freaky; I never go there." Her personal tipping point was probably when they ripped out natural habitat to bring in exotic plants and animals for Disney's Animal Kingdom: "I have to drive around with blinders now." I hear that so much, I wonder if we aren't all wearing them. Which would explain a lot.

With great affection, Jeannie describes her circle of friends as "these wild-eyed radical activists." She is not trying to fit into somebody else's idea of the mainstream, spiritually or any other way: "My bible is a book called *The Great Cosmic Mother*. I have it in a very special place in my house." Yet recent events have convinced her that moderation might not be such a dirty word after all. There is so much at stake that symbolic stands no longer appeal, and she has lost all enthusiasm for the Green Party. "I went to a convention, and there was a clothing-optional place," she says, and covers her face with her hands. "And that's okay, if that's where you are. But that's not the way to win over the most people."

For Katherine Harris, it seems too late for that, and the bad news keeps on coming. Campaign staffers appear to be jumping out of the windows holding hands—fortunately, her HQ is on the first floor—but I'm curious about the women who are sticking by her and, in short, trying to make that work. Are they feeling sorry for her, too? Her campaign office in Tampa is a cavernous, mostly empty space strewn with boxes and campaign signs. On one wall, there is the usual poster-size photo of the candidate, and on another, a large framed picture of a little blond girl in a red, white, and blue tulle tutu, holding a magic wand. The receptionist waves at me, then goes back to examining her French manicure and talking on the phone: "He says he keeps calling and you don't answer. He's" —she looks up at me—"he's, uh, not very happy." Then the press secretary, Chris Ingram, comes to collect me and introduces me to two young Harris for Senate aides, Jenna Lihvarcik and Ashley Fishburn. Both are recent college grads, both are twenty-two years old. Neither seems to feel she is on some mission of mercy.

Ashley, who looks like a model and double-majored in political science and Spanish, can express her purpose here in a few words: "I was protesting at abortion clinics as a five-year-old. I was never arrested—my father was, though; he has a record—and it was exciting, and that's what fueled my passion. I just want to change the world." At this, her friend Jenna, who resembles the hyper-competent sidekick Chloe on TV's *24,* emits a groan of self-deprecation: "Maybe I should have gone first." Or not.

Ashley continues, "As a five-year-old, you don't know what's going on. I just knew we were protesting something bad." But now, she says, she sees opposing abortion rights as a feminist issue. "Abortion kills, and you hear these male legislators say, 'Personally, I'm opposed, but . . .' and I think that's wrong, and if there were more women in government, you wouldn't have that. We're grossly underrepresented because women don't run for office. They put family first, which is good, but maybe they have been disenfranchised in being told to do that. From what I've observed in the last five months, it's a good old boys' network." Chris, the press secretary, adds that the coverage has been incredibly sexist: "The media is fixated, and when it's a woman . . . I get calls all the time from very respectable media asking what designer she was wearing. And I say, 'When did you ask Senator Frist that?'" Maybe if Senator Frist dressed better? No one laughs.

Jenna, who grew up in New Jersey, interned for a couple of Democratic state lawmakers there, "and I really liked the people even though I'm a Republican." Her dad was president of his local Rotary Club and got her involved in civic life early on, as a volunteer for Habitat for Humanity. So, would she maybe like to run for office herself? She smiles. "I wouldn't mind working for Ashley when she runs." That's not "if" but "when"; Ashley has been scoping out local races since her junior year. "I'm the oldest, so I've set a high standard for my sisters," she says, "and they despise me for it." I might not want to pitch in alongside these young women, but they know what they believe, and they are in there selling it, even when nobody's buying. So if, in the long run, it is the former kindergartener abortion protesters who carry the day, nobody who isn't doing likewise can complain. By the time I leave, I am not feeling sorry for their boss anymore.

Women Ashley and Jenna's age overwhelmingly favor the Democrats, but a local party stalwart, Mary Jane Arrington, the only female county commissioner in neighboring Osceola County's 128-year history, says she can't help but feel her side is doing a lousy job of capitalizing on that advantage. "On all of our local advisory boards, they're all baby boomers and older, so I'm concerned about these Generation X- and Y-ers. They're perfectly capable, and you have to embrace them with their piercings and tattoos. They want to wear shorts to work, but that doesn't mean they're not capable."

Mary Jane was voted out of office in '02, and I gather she has no more designs on public office. "Why do people come here" to overbuild and crowd the highways? she asks when I arrive in Kissimmee, late and muttering about congestion on I-4. "To me, it's not pretty, and why live by a major theme park?" She is an urban planner, and the street her office is on used to be lovely and tree-lined, she says, until Hurricane Charley whipped through in 2004. Central Florida used to be considered safe from hurricane damage, too, "but global warming is real," and storms are becoming more intense.

When I mention that the alligator situation is also a little unnerving, she does not exactly offer reassurance: "This *is* a phenomenon, three women in ten days. And you are talking enormous gators—eight or nine feet long—and people don't know that they can run thirty-five miles an hour. I skied over one one time." She does give me a tip: Forget snout-punching and poke 'em in the eye. Maybe I should be walking around armed with my umbrella *and* my car key?

She does not think the race she lost in '02 was in any way rigged: Voter turnout was 80 percent for Republicans and 50 percent for the Democrats. So, though Democrats outnumber Republicans in the county, she came up short. She thinks election shenanigans had something to do with that outcome indirectly, because so many Democrats have concluded since 2000 that their votes may or may not count for anything.

She was one of those county officials you saw on TV during the recount, holding the ballots up to the light. For Florida Democrats, that was a moment as well preserved in memory as where they were when Kennedy was shot or when the planes hit the Twin Towers. "We were at the elections office, and the polls hadn't even closed yet, and they were calling it for Bush. Then people in the Panhandle said when they heard that, they weren't going" to the polls. "The state constitution says if you lose by half a percentage point, you have the right to a hand recount of the whole state." Why Gore's team asked for only a partial recount, only of the "undervotes," only in some counties, is to her an enduring mystery: "We couldn't count the 'overvotes,' where you punched Al Gore and then also wrote in his name. We couldn't look at the clear intent. That was not what we had been asked to do." And if she does not take solace, exactly, in Katherine Harris's current predicament, she can appreciate the spectacle. "Sometimes," she says, grinning, "paybacks are hell."

Her greatest fear for '08 is that another polarizing female, Hillary Clinton, will be her party's nominee. "I think Bill Clinton could get reelected, but I don't think Hillary can, and I hope she's smart enough to know that. She is smart, but she comes across as a pushy woman. She's not the right one, and to break the glass ceiling, you have to be the right one." The most appealing thing about Hillary has always been her enemies, who often seem not in their right mind, screaming that she is a murderer and calling her names like "Her Thighness." They make you *want* to like her.

In Washington, one does hear lots of pro-Hillary talk, mostly from people who worked in the Clinton administration. But of all the women I talked to for this book, the number who said they thought she might be "the right one" wasn't hard to tally, because it was zero. It would be hard to say whether it is conservatives or liberals—who consider her a sellout, especially on Iraq—who mind her more intensely at this point. But the feeling they have in common is "Anybody but Hillary." And only in that way, I'm afraid, is she any more of a "uniter, not a divider," than the act she'd like to follow. Those in the political middle said they either just don't care for her or feel she has no chance of being elected. Often, their objections to her boiled down to the nagging feeling that she is simply not sincere—a qualm that any attempt at repositioning or repackaging seems likely to reinforce.

(I thought I finally had one for the Hillary Bandwagon, right here in Tampa, when I saw that Ann May, a friend of Thalia's, had an old campaign snapshot of the senator on her refrigerator. She denied it, though: "I like Hillary, but I'm afraid she'd be the only one who could keep the Democrats from winning. She'd draw so many people out to vote against her that wouldn't come out otherwise." So another no vote, despite the fact that it was Bill Clinton's impeachment that made Ann "realize I was a Democrat" relatively late in life, in her fifties. "I think I was happier before I got so involved in politics, and I do not believe Bush was elected president in 2000. I live here, and I'm telling you, we did not go for Bush. . . .")

After Mary Jane lost her race in '02, she remembers her youngest son's girlfriend telling her she sure was sorry. "And I said, 'Kristen, did you vote?' and she said no!" That son, Brandon Arrington, is planning to run for Mary Jane's old seat on the board of county commissioners in the next election, and his girlfriend, Kristen Aston, who had never voted before, wouldn't dream of missing an election now. She has not registered as a Democrat, though, but as an Independent. Over a beer at the Friday's in front of my hotel, she makes clear that she opposes pretty much every move the Bush administration has ever made. Why is she not a registered Democrat? "If the Democrats right now had more of a message or a plan" beyond just opposing the president, she says, then maybe.

Kristen is a striking redhead who made her living as a dancer in Vegas and Aruba, where "I danced in a drag-queen show" before moving back home to Kissimmee. Now she sells real estate and is as disturbed as anybody by the "ick" factor in popular culture. On weekends, she judges dance competitions that she says have changed some since her days as a contestant. "In Miami they have all these saucy eight-year-olds with costumes cut down to here and salsa heels, and they're working it like they know how to, and you're like, 'This is so wrong.'" She doesn't see a lot that is to her taste in politics, either: "What turns me off about Hillary is I don't feel the realness from her."

Kristen did vote for John Kerry, whom she met at a rally and asked to sign her A VILLAGE IN TEXAS IS MISSING ITS IDIOT T-shirt. But watching him during the campaign truly saddened her. "I wanted him to say the war was wrong. I saw footage of when he came back from Vietnam with all this passion, but after all those years in the Senate, where did it go?" In fact, the only two politicians Kristen mentions favorably are Republicans, South Carolina senator Lindsey Graham, who she thinks is so good at challenging the president that "Brandon has joked that he's my boyfriend," and California governor Arnold Schwarzenegger. "I like that he's spoken out against Republicans," she says. "He does what he wants, and I admire his style." Kristen's mother, who was widowed last year, has never been politically active but will be, Kristen is sure, now that Brandon is planning to run for office. "She thinks of herself as a Republican, but that's just a lack of education." I hate to tell her, but spoken like a Democrat.

Another new voter I meet here is Betty Bowers, a fifty-five-year-old African-American woman who works for the public employees union and never even registered until a couple of years ago. She grew up near Orlando, and her parents picked oranges all their lives—until, at age sixty-two, her mother took a job as a school custodian in Lake County so she could work toward a small pension and get some health insurance. "I don't know if they ever voted or not," Betty says, spinning her cell phone around on her office's conference room table as she talks. "That was just a discussion that didn't happen in my house."

Betty got married right out of high school and moved to Connecticut, where she and her husband joined the Jehovah's Witnesses, a church that discourages voting as too worldly. As she sees it now, "It was a control thing" for her husband to coax her into the church, "but they're very disciplined, and we did everything together, and it kept the kids out of trouble. When I'm out now, I can see who is a Jehovah's Witness just by how the kids behave. My daughter was sick in a meeting once, and she did not *move*."

It was scary at first, knocking on doors to proselytize, she says, "but I learned a lot about people, that everybody's the same with the same issues. Wealthy or on welfare, everyone wants love, and it's all about families—all the love, the hate, the discipline, it all comes out there. I found out that softness and meekness defuse people; when you don't yell back, they don't know what to do. But I cuss people now," she says, smiling, and gives the cell phone another spin. "I'm not that meek girl anymore."

When she divorced, left the church, and moved back to Florida over twenty years ago, she went to work as a police dispatcher but still didn't register to vote until she got involved in union politics at the department. "I got so excited. You don't know it, but everything is politics, and I didn't see it that way before." In '04, Kerry and Edwards visited here—the parking lot right outside the union office building—and Betty heard both of them speak. "I didn't know anything about them, but I said, 'I like *that* guy,' and they said, 'That's not Kerry, that's Edwards.' I was so green, but everything he said, I knew he would either do or die trying. We need someone more like that."

Betty's husband—whom she remarried two years ago, after they had spent decades apart—has meanwhile become an equally convinced Republican, one who "gets up and it's Hannity and Colmes twenty-four/seven. And I'll tell you why he became a Republican: He went down to vote, and the lady said, 'Oh, you're a Democrat,'" apparently assuming that because he's black, "and handed him a Democratic ballot. "And he said, 'Why do you think that? I'm a Republican.' Now he *loves* Bush, and I say, 'If I would have known you were a Republican, I never would have remarried you.' I just think he fell and hit his head."

I get lost again on my way from Betty's to an evening meeting of the Pasco County Black Women's Democratic Club way out in Wesley Chapel, where the citrus groves meet suburban sprawl. I have to call in so many times for navigational aid that I feel like I know everybody by the time I come in the door. First, I'm dying to know which of the half-dozen women who've turned out at Blanche Benford's tonight has the W. sticker on her bumper. But it turns out, it came that way—used car.

Just the mention of the president's name provokes this from the hostess: "I don't think Bush won it; it was stolen, and unless we push for paper ballots, we won't ever win here again." Blanche, who is sixty-one and remembers when her mother couldn't vote because she couldn't afford the five-dollar poll tax, says things are not done by the book even in her local polling place. "The first thing I see is this long table with Republican stuff on it," in clear violation of the law. "I sure did get on my cell phone and report it, but people were picking it up. And those exit polls have never been wrong before, so why this year? Because they stole the election! I was upset with the Democrats behind that, and I was upset when Kerry conceded." He didn't have the stomach for the fight the voters deserved, the way she saw it.

But voters have also been discouraged far too easily, she thinks, ever since that fiasco in 2000. Take the '04 municipal election in neighboring Zephyrhills—"City of Pure Water"—where a city council candidate who ran on a platform of changing that town's Martin Luther King Avenue back to Sixth Avenue won by just eighty-five votes—and promptly did get the street name changed. Yet after months of turmoil over the issue, and protests that made the national news, only twenty-seven of the more than five hundred black voters registered there bothered to turn out for that election, Blanche says. That's how hopeless people are.

Blanche's daughter, Cece Estelle, is still ticked off at them for staying home on Election Day. "It's not optional! I'm very proud to be black, but I'm bitter with my own people" over that. Cece works for the Florida Department of Children and Families, then pulls a midnight shift at Wal-Mart. At both places, she sees families working so hard for so little, unable even to get health insurance. "How can we sit around and not be outraged?" Her mom harumphs at that and answers that the president's power is so unchecked that at this point, "Every day that I wake up and we're not under martial law is a good day."

Another thing Cece says she cannot get her arms around is why it seems as though it's the best-off Americans who are not only the most favored but also the most resentful. In her day job, she says, she meets a lot of "seniors who are well-to-do but want to keep their money and not spend it on a nursing home, so they want to get on Medicaid," which is harder to do under the new rules. "One man, he got so mad, and he was a Republican. I said, 'Well, who do you think is in office?' But they didn't mean to piss off those people. That's their base."

Angella Bowman, a fellow party activist who is not African-American, says she thinks most working people are too exhausted to get all worked up. "Trying to get people to volunteer, I say, 'How about Saturday?' And they say, 'That's the only day I can take my kids to softball.' People are tired."

"And selfish," adds Blanche's younger sister, Mary Earl, who just retired from her social work job in Minnesota and moved here. She says she can't bear to look at the president but does want to know what he says, "So when he's on TV, I buy the newspaper." As for the war, don't get her started. "In ten years, we'll have all the Iraqis here," trying to make it up to them for having destroyed their country, just like we did for the Vietnamese. "And we'll give them all fifteen thousand dollars," Blanche says. "So they can have a nail shop."

Culturally, these women are conservative. "It can't possibly be a Christian nation when the value system is completely backward and it's all youth and beauty," complains Cece, even if she is forty-three and luminous, with the skin of a twelve-year-old. "The whole thing of flaunting your body really scares me. This is one sick, perverted country." She and her mother and her aunt all oppose abortion rights, gay marriage, and careless language on TV. They want Twain and Shakespeare taught in school, and say nothing makes them madder than hearing Democrats called godless. Crucially, they see Republican positions on all these matters as strategic rather than sincere.

When Blanche says, "If I see two men or two women together, it does turn me; I do get sick at my stomach," Angella offers a softer view: "I prefer that *everybody* keep their displays to themselves." Angella is also far more optimistic than her African-American friends about their party's prospects. She is pumped about Howard Dean's fifty-state plan and the way the Florida Democratic Party is going to win in '08 by getting all the faithful to bring in ten new voters each.

She leaves early, and the rest of us keep talking and picking at the cheese plate until it is almost time for Cece's midnight shift.

Blanche shakes her head. "Even if we all get ten people—or twenty—it's not going to matter if the count's not right. I've been out there trying to convince people to vote, talking to ten or fifteen young black guys sitting playing cards under a tree. And I'm telling you, nothing we've been talking about has anything to do with them." Young men like that, with no jobs and few prospects, would have to move a few rungs up the economic ladder, Blanche says, even to get to the next level of challenge for the Democrats, which is "to convince people that we're not in cahoots with Katherine Harris"—unwilling to so much as raise the possibility of electoral theft in broad daylight.

Crossing Over with John Edwards, and Other Rescue Fantasies

"I didn't feel complete at the end."

The first time I saw John Edwards work a room, in Iowa in the winter of 2003, I could hardly wait to phone in the news: "This is Bill Clinton with his pants on!" were, I am afraid, my exact words to my editor at *Newsweek*. Women in Iowa—and they were mostly women, as I look back—heard when he talked, and they responded extravagantly, with tears and testimonials and comparisons to Bobby Kennedy, though they were hardly political neophytes. For the record, one thing I did not hear was a lot of talk about the senator's looks; it's the listening thing that makes men attractive to women, that and the impression that, as men of taste and vision, they like us. My friend Lynn Hunter, who lives in Ames, where her husband is a professor of theology at Iowa State, is only 97 percent joking when she talks about the significant eye contact Edwards lavished on her during a speech he gave on campus. "He sought me out in the room and spoke directly to me; that's why I got a Christmas card."

I may not be the world's hardest sell; I am the reporter who enjoyed hearing Al Gore explain fractals in 2000, if that tells you anything, and if I live to see the last glacier melt into a snow cone,

I will never get over what happened to him then. Across the ideological spectrum, I tend to like the funny ducks who go into politics; they live in an irregular world and work like maniacs to maintain their place in it, often because they are ill suited to other employment, slightly at sea in the private sphere and actually trying to contribute if they can. Not so unlike the people in my business, in other words, though we can never be friends.

Doubtless, too, Edwards seemed extra engaging alongside poor woebegone John Kerry. Whenever I see Kerry, I am reminded of what a friend who frequently found herself stuck behind him at the salad bar in the Senate dining room once told me: He'd stand there forever, selecting each perfect pea and sprout one at a time—though in the end, he always seemed to walk away disappointed, with barely enough greens on his plate to keep a model alive.

Full-blown political dork crushes are as dangerous as any other infatuation, of course, and, if anything, even less likely to end well. Yet everywhere I go, I hear women who should know better thinking out loud about The One—the candidate who has it all. And for those of us who are not Republicans, the fixer-upper template for these rescue fantasies is invariably Hillary's husband.

Whenever I mention Edwards in Washington, people always say, "Elizabeth is great, isn't she?" And his wife is wonderful. But I liked that he talked about race in every single setting. I liked that he showed some passion on the subject of our *moral* obligation to the have-nots in our country, and brought clarity to every topic he touched: "It's just not that complicated," he'd say, and what a relief that was. I liked that when our family was watching him speak about basic fairness on TV one night, I could say to the kids, *"This* is why we are Democrats."

His unglamorous priorities could not possibly be poll-driven . . . could they? Which, ever open to fresh disillusion, is how I wind up deciding to check out his between-political-campaigns anti-poverty campaign. I hear women say they wish he had been the nominee in '04, but was his appeal a fleeting one or something sturdier? Does a platform informed by an old-fashioned bleeding heart retain any allure to us? And if this guy isn't *the* guy, does he have anything the guy can learn from when he finally shows up?

"I keep waiting for him to actually *do* something," the young woman sitting behind me in the snack bar of the University of North Carolina's law library in Chapel Hill is saying to her friend, talking about Edwards. I'm there to hear a speech he is to give that September day, not long after the semester has started, in his new position as the director of the school's Center on Poverty, Work and Opportunity. The girl's friend laughs and pretends to address Edwards: "You want to eliminate poverty? Okay, get out of your job" and make room for someone who needs the paycheck.

I don't hear the rest but take my seat in the atrium where Edwards is to speak, and soon enough, he ambles forward, tan and relaxed, with his hands in his pockets. He asks that we focus on the nearly one in four children who live in poverty in the United States, a state of affairs he calls this "the greatest moral issue in our country today," even more obviously so now that Katrina has blown the lid off the lie that Bush's America has nothing to apologize for. "The truth is," he says, "the people who suffer the most from Katrina are the same people who suffer the most every day. In this moment, it's so important to remember that they are part of us. Is your success just your success and your failure yours alone? It's not true. I didn't get here by myself, and those who are struggling didn't, either."

I always liked this part of his stump speech—and because no Democrat has been willing to talk this way in such a long time, am downright grateful. But the questions from the audience, about micro-loans and land use and global poverty, are well beyond where the speaker is ready to go, at least for now. And when we talk afterward, in his office, Edwards says pretty much the same thing all over again. "The press, when I'm talking about poverty, they're like this," he says, looking all around, then up at the sky, like a three-year-old on a soccer field. "They want to say, 'Oh, he's mobilizing his base' or something. Whereas it's more like, 'If I'm going down, this is how I want to go down.'"

He tells me, "I don't know if I'll ever run again" for any office, "but there's no downside" to running against poverty in the meantime, "except that it runs completely contrary to the instincts of most lifelong politicians." He might know a little more than he lets on about such instincts, and despite all his talk about boldness, is excruciatingly careful, even in near-complete eclipse, to say almost everything of interest off the record.

He does say one thing about his decision to focus on this issue that stays with me: "I used to get in arguments with other lawyers all the time. I'd argue that the *first* thing you tell the jury is the problem with your case. Then they trust you." Sort of like the saleswoman who gently breaks it to you that Dress A really does not maximize your charms, so that when she is awed by how you look in Dress B, you're more apt to believe her? Exactly, he says.

For some reason, this puts me in mind of the advice an extremely successful colleague once gave me: You can never flatter anyone too outrageously, because even if they suspect you're having them on, they won't know for sure and will like it anyway—which kind of took the sugar out of all subsequent compliments from her. But is Edwards really winking that once you nail sincerity, everything else is a curtain call? I'm not sure, but either way, I am not flattered to have been let in on this particular piece of stagecraft. You have to know your jury to play to it.

Still, I remain eager to catch part of his anti-poverty Opportunity Rocks Tour of college campuses and meet up with him on the last leg. Before the day's main event at the University of Michigan, he makes an early-morning stop at a neighborhood agency called Motor City Blight Busters in Detroit, in what until recently had been a warehouse in the Old Redford district, right next door to the Redford Theatre, the very last movie theater in the city of Detroit. (Now showing: *Invasion of the Body Snatchers*.) Volunteers have turned the warehouse into a trendy-looking neighborhood art gallery, café, and studio where they offer kids free art lessons in the summer. They have also been busy knocking down crack houses and creating "peace parks," restoring more than 150 homes so run-down they'd been unoccupied, and building almost two hundred new ones.

This morning at seven A.M., some young women from the U of M are already at work out back, shoveling rocks and sweeping up debris, preparing the property for the construction of a new patio area. One of the students raking trash, Rachel Pultusker, knows exactly what she's looking for in her next president: "I want someone who understands the problems schools face and has worked in under-resourced schools. Detroit has a fairly negative image around the country, but people care—that's the point—and I want someone who sees value in that. I'm only twenty-one and have only voted once, but I'm in the communities that are our country's biggest challenge three or four times a week, so to see someone on TV" spouting catchphrases doesn't catch it.

Edwards shows up just then and introduces himself around, though none of the young women stops working to go inside and hear him. After a short tour, he sits down with the founder of the agency, John George, with local TV cameras rolling. John is a former insurance salesman who got so fed up with his city's failure to do anything about a crack house right around the corner from him that one day when the drug dealers were out, he got some plywood and paint, went over to the place, and started boarding it up and painting it himself, cutting the grass for good measure. Some of his neighbors saw what he was doing and came out and joined in, and when the dealers saw the new deal, he says, they moved on and never came back.

What he did with that crack house became the model for Motor City Blight Busters, which he started on a card table in his basement eighteen years ago. A few of his most recent success stories are here this morning to shake the senator's hand, including a young woman from the neighborhood who owns two businesses now. A single mom tells how "I see these people here outside working and tearing down houses. I come outside and become a part of it, and they help me get a house with a nice backyard for my kids. I've never seen anybody like these people; they are *doin'* it. Somebody still believes." A local artist who has been painting murals on buildings all over the neighborhood reports that not one of them has been tagged with graffiti, but some forty kids who've watched him working have become regulars at his art-appreciation classes. "It's *so* important to create points of light in places like this," Edwards tells the founder, right before the TV crew packs up. At least he got them to come.

Then Edwards sits down with a couple of student journalists from *The Michigan Daily*. "You're trying to get kids involved in fighting poverty and involved in politics in general?" one of them asks. "The former, not the latter," he answers. Okay. "But things like raising the minimum wage seem more like just repairing the problem. Do you have any ideas for ending poverty?"

"I do," he says, but does not elaborate. "I'm worried the attention will dissipate" after the startling images of poverty in New Orleans fade from memory in the public consciousness. "Politicians in Washington have not done anything about it for decades, and I want to start a grassroots movement—and this was *my* idea, not somebody who works for me, but *me*." At this point, the young interviewers are looking at him like, "Congratu-bloomin'-lations, Bub," but he doesn't seem to notice. It seems not to have occurred to him that they never would have assumed otherwise, or found the idea of a politician with a thought of his own quite as extraordinary as he apparently does.

By now, I'm acquainted with the talking points, so in the van on the way to the event in Ann Arbor, we chat as he makes his way through his McBreakfast. (Would even Churchill have seemed Churchillian to anyone who'd watched him take his morning Tater Tots? One thinks not.) Edwards tells a funny story about his wife correcting his grammar at a big-deal dinner party in Manhattan, and adds that he has me pegged as maybe a little bit of a slave to *Strunk & White* myself, no? And proves that my colleague was right about flattery; who wouldn't enjoy being compared to Elizabeth?

As we arrive in Ann Arbor, he predicts I'll be amazed by what I'm about to witness. "The most inspiring thing is after, when people in droves come up and say, 'I want to help; just tell us what to do.'" And "it really is true that college students are more focused on the important things. They're not asking little questions— Oh, what about this?" he asks an aide, interrupting himself to hold up for her approval a fleece jacket that's more collegiate-looking than the suit coat he had been wearing.

It's over an hour before he's to speak, but the Diag in front of the library is already filling with students dressed for the Arctic and willing to wait in the cold sunshine. A young woman walking away from the crowd is telling a friend, "The e-mails I got were like, 'Oh, come, because MTV is going to be there, blah, blah, blah.'" But there are some serious-minded kids on the quad. "I want to do my duty and help the world," says Demita Brown, a senior biology major who plans to become a doctor after a stint in the Peace Corps and has skipped micro to be here. "We talk about politics all the time in my apartment, and talk about the news. I want to see change, and you can't just say you disagree. My dad is like, 'You're black and you're female and you'd better pay attention to politics.'"

Edwards bounds down the library steps to an energetic welcome, and after greetings and thanks, he begins, "Please, don't leave here without signing up so we can stay in touch. . . . This movement—which is what this is—was not somebody else's idea. It was *my* idea," he says, and the crowd seems to think he's making a joke, because they give him a big laugh. He tells several stories about Katrina survivors he met recently at a shelter in Baton Rouge, and one man who went out at five every morning to look for day work, though he hadn't been hired yet.

"Now there are a million more people in poverty than there were a year ago," Edwards tells the crowd. "This is not complicated; it's wrong. They're just lazy? It's a lie! Most are women and most are working, responsibly taking care of their kids, up against extraordinary barriers, but they keep trying! I wake up in the middle of the night with their faces in my head. They are desperate for a champion—and it's not me, it's you. I can go across the country preaching the gospel, but they need you, because it's clear they can't count on politicians in Washington.

"My father, who never went to college a day, is worth every bit as much as me, and as any president of the United States—particularly the one we've got right now," Edwards says, and the line gets the biggest cheer of the day. Then he asks them to be sure and sign the "Opportunity Rocks Pledge" to perform at least twenty hours of volunteer work over the next year. Across campus, chimes begin to ring and are immediately drowned out by the Journey song "Don't Stop Believin'."

At the front of the crowd are two young women from near Joliet, Illinois, who have driven all night to be here, starting out right after they got off work at Office Depot. "He's the only one I've seen who has a genuine interest to getting through to people our age," says one of them, Jill Hastings, who is nineteen. "We live in New Lenox, Illinois, center of social apathy, so we had to drive out here" for a little hit of activism. Her friend, Sara Bechtold, who's twenty, laughs and says, "When we said we were coming to see John Edwards, people were like, 'The psychic?'" (They had assumed Jill and Sara were off for a séance with the medium John Edward, who used to put people in touch with their dead relatives on his now departed Sci Fi show, *Crossing Over with John Edward*.)

Sara was first in line to vote at her precinct on Election Day, "and our close circle of friends are involved, but most people are apathetic because our leaders don't go out of their way to speak to them." Yeah, but "if people our age did get involved," Jill says, "they'd realize how screwed we are. It's easier for them to be ignorant."

By now the song that's blasting is—oh no, can it be?—the old Clinton theme song, "Don't Stop (Thinking about Tomorrow)," and the guy who'd like to be the next Southerner to win the White House is mobbed by young women holding up their cell phones to take his picture. A couple of freshmen walking away from Edwards are jumping up and down as they review the shots they got. "It hit home how he said poverty affects women," says one of them, Sejal Patel, who is from Okemos, Michigan. "The election didn't work out in his favor, but he still feels it's his duty to talk about this, and that's very admirable." Her friend Freya Motafram, from Brookfield, Wisconsin, says she's going to sign the pledge to volunteer. "It's not much, but if everybody did it, it would make a difference." But another friend of theirs, Renee Mitchell, from South Lyon, Michigan, says she did *not* appreciate what she heard, not at all. "I thought it was very unprofessional of him. He *had* to put the dig in towards the president. It was fine, his message about community service, but I don't believe in what he's saying."

"What?" Sejal asks her. "You don't believe in helping poor people?"

"With the deficit so low," Renee argues, "I don't feel like that's necessary" for the government to be shelling out money to help kids go to college.

"With the deficit so high, you mean?"

"Right. I just think Bush is a very good president, and I'm satisfied with the way the war is going." A couple of other young women have joined us, and at this, all of them jump in at once: "WMDs. . . . lowest approval rating. . . . not just liberals." Been there, girls.

"Well, I believe there *were* WMDs," Renee insists, holding her ground. "We had the intelligence. And sometimes you just have to show people." As I'm scribbling, she says to me, "Put this down: 'President Bush, I am your Number One Fan. I don't believe in free handouts.'" So, one of her friends asks, then how does she swing tuition? "My parents are helping me," she answers. By the time I back out of the conversation, it has turned into a full-scale argument.

Nearby, two friends who are already committed volunteers are in complete agreement about the speech. "It was good, but there was a lack of direction," says one of them, Rachel Arndt. "He needed to give people an avenue, a way to mobilize, and what organizations to go through" rather than tossing out generalities and collecting e-mail addresses. So Opportunity Rocks was an opportunity wasted, says her friend Jignesha Patel, who the night before also decided to join the Peace Corps after graduation. "I just hoped to see more organization, and felt like there could have been so much more; I didn't feel complete at the end. I work doing this all year long, and no one can be JFK, but his passion and his diligence *made* the Peace Corps, and that's what I'd like to see Opportunity Rocks be. It seemed to me like, 'Maybe I'm going to run for president again someday, so let's do *something*.' But if you'd really spent eight or nine months in the community, you'd have more to say."

Unfortunately, I am with Jignesha; this was not Al Gore on global warming, OK? But I am also kind of annoyed with myself for noticing. I carp that the Democrats are too stuck in their heads even to know how to play on the emotional level where elections are won and lost. But then here is this fired-up guy, saying all the right things in simple, declarative sentences, and now I'm wishing he could get some complexity going? And even for a minute there, clucking to myself that perhaps there was a reason old pea-picking Kerry was at the top of the ticket after all? Maybe this, too, is why we lose: We are never satisfied.

The crowd has dissipated by then, and as advertised, Edwards is meeting a crew from MTV. In the elevator on the way to join up with them, an aide supplies Edwards with the name of the reporter who'll be doing the interview. "Who?" he asks, and she repeats it. "He interviewed you in New Hampshire in the general."

"Hey, nice to see you again," he calls to the guy a few seconds later. "I was just trying to think when it was we did our last thing."

"I just looked it up, and it was a year ago yesterday," the reporter says, terribly pleased. "Different times."

"Yes, different times," Edwards echoes. "The most important goal is to start a movement, and not among politicians. I can see on your face you don't think politicians are real people. . . . The response of these kids is very real, though." After the interview, the reporter walks Edwards to his car and, before tucking him into the front seat, says, "Let us know if you decide to run."

"Maybe we ought to let you announce it this time," Edwards tells him, grinning, and the car pulls away. The trip, it's true, has not been all I'd hoped. Not only is Edwards probably not the guy, there probably is no guy. Still, I come away oddly exhilarated, and I think that's because so many of the young women I've met seem a lot like that John George of the Motor City Blight Busters, ready to step in, not only in cleaning out crack houses but in cleaning house in our government, so that we can believe in it again.

Everybody knows that great husbands are made, not born,

and maybe it's not so different when it comes to finding The One in political life. If Bush has proved anything, it's surely that we don't need the perfect candidate to succeed. We could use better candidates, yes. But we might need more fully engaged voters even more.

Women of the Storm

*"I couldn't go back to playing
a lot of tennis and exercising."*

Anybody who thinks they can top Anne Milling in graciousness is mistaken, that's all. When I arrive at her Uptown home, she is just back from hand-delivering a few thank-you notes to friends who had attended her son's wedding a couple of days earlier, "people who had been so wonderful I didn't want to wait." She apologizes for her casual clothes. "I did not even get dressed today," she chides herself, though honestly, she could fly up front and the only glance she'd get would be for looking good. She seats me, hydrates me, and heaps praise upon all mutual acquaintances. Leaning into the conversation in her sunny library off the pool, she wants to hear all about me, too, and wonders if I think running a full-page ad in *The Washington Post* to thank all those members of Congress who have come down to see the Katrina damage firsthand would be too obvious a prod to those who have not yet made the trip. "Would that be *too* rude?"

When she takes off the white gloves, you see, the effect is magnified. And the love train does come to a head-jerking halt on the subject of elected officials, on all levels and in both parties: "We need to start with a clean slate," she says briskly, and ticks off the various strategic errors everyone from the mayor to the president has made—not in the immediate aftermath of the hurricanes, mind you, but in all the time they've had since then to make up for the early rounds of dereliction.

Meantime, Anne has pulled together Women of the Storm—130 highly motivated women who flew to Washington in January 2006 to invite members of Congress to survey the storm damage for themselves before voting down any more aid packages. "The men aren't going to do this. They don't like to nag and badger, and we do. King"—that's her husband—"says, 'Oh my *God,* you stormy women.'" Formidable as she is, though, this is not one of those old-fashioned made-for-TV tales where the heroine—Dina Merrill, I think, whom Anne resembles—rallies the gals and rebuilds their town by the end of the second hour.

Nothing is as it was, and even those who have been able to stay on—and have to acknowledge how lucky they are, on top of it—have been changed. Not gently, over time, but all at once, when the levees didn't hold. So I've come here hoping to learn how all the women of the storm are processing their new reality, political and otherwise. After all that has happened, the role of government in everyday life could hardly be less academic. Or chaos theory, with connections we never noticed before suddenly made apparent. And it takes time to sort through all that destruction on this scale has dredged up.

I was here right after Katrina, but even after everything I've read about the relaxed pace of repairs in the seven months since then, am staggered to see all that has not happened. The highways are still so littered with the carcasses of cars that they hardly register after a while, like squashed bugs on the windshield. There are so many street signs down that it's hard to navigate outside the French Quarter. And really, what would it take to fix the traffic lights? Just blocks from the Quarter, there is nothing but gray from ground to sky, and parts of the Ninth Ward look like Dresden after the war. Vast swaths of ruined cityscape handily illustrate the "heckuva job" this whole administration has done—while its officials keep repeating, as often as necessary, that absolutely everything is under control. It was that disconnect, I think, between the live shots of mayhem and the familiar assurances that help was not only on the way but had already arrived, that was harder to take than any of the other failures. "Who knew?" just didn't work as well after Katrina as it had for so long in Iraq; we'd heard it once too often, and begun to wonder whether it might not be better to put people with less contempt for government in charge of it next time.

Not that anybody here much wants to see their hometown turned into a symbol—of either the cost of cronyism or the way that believing government can't do anything right tends to become self-fulfilling. They simply want their city back, and they know that's not going to happen anytime soon. After spending only a few days talking to people still living in trailers in somebody's driveway, I'm beginning to wonder if it will happen at all. Our Lord did say, "The poor you will always have with you," but it is the lowest-income areas of New Orleans that sit empty. A couple of African-American leaders have called the result a de facto ethnic cleansing, and it is a political cleansing for sure, with much of the city's underclass—Democrats, in the main—still and perhaps forever relocated. New Orleanians of means miss them, and not only in the ways they might have predicted.

The enormity of what New Orleanians are facing now is such that it looks almost like the end of politics; people are too mad and forlorn to be partisans of anything. The yard sign you see everywhere says THROW THEM ALL OUT, but it is not clear if the residents who remain have the energy for that, or would see any of the likely replacements as much of an improvement. In fact, if there is a Katrina effect, it is that people here see all the button-pushing machinations of our political system with such awful clarity that I would not want to be the first candidate post-Katrina to try a typical "Too Liberal for Louisiana" ad campaign, with Mary Landrieu morphing into Satan. Voters know they have been abandoned, so what promises can be made? And yet, abandoned, they are banding together.

One morning, I'm talking to a local dermatologist, Sharon Meyer, in the new office she's recently moved into. Her old building, adjacent to Memorial Medical Center—the hospital where forty-five bodies were found when the waters receded—flooded in the storm. And the first thing she has to say about all the upheaval is "There's nobody here anymore to run the city, and we all need those people to be our lawn boys."

With Katrina bearing down, she says, "I evacuated with two pairs of pants just like everybody else" and, with her family, decamped to San Antonio for four months. Her business is still off by about a third, and another third of the patients she does see fly in for their Botox or dermabrasion from Houston, where a lot of them have relocated. "It's only a matter of time before I lose them, too," she says, "once they get comfortable in their new town." Still, her receptionists are asking for three dollars more an hour because they have to drive in from so much farther out. Four of her five employees have quit in the last month, and not one of her old routines has survived intact. "I love my little workout on Tuesday mornings, and my trainer still doesn't have his power back on; he has to shower at the gym. When I drop off my laundry now, it's like a three-week wait. Those of us who are lucky enough to have a nanny or a personal assistant at home, I get her to stand in line. But other people, it's stressing us out. You survive on adrenaline at first. But now you're saying, 'Okay, this is my life.'"

Now, the temptation off the top is to wince at the lawn-boy thing and maybe even think, "My God, woman, people died." But as it turns out, I am the one who needs a reminder—that no one here needs any reminders. Because the first thing out of a woman's mouth is not necessarily *the* thing, you know? When I've listened a little longer, I start to think that this might be the thing: "Two out of three doctors have left the city, and my neighbor who was a dermatologist, too, committed suicide. She had three kids, just like I do, and her husband's an orthopedist," as Sharon's is. "And she was so determined"—here Sharon looks right at me, I guess so as not to look away—"that she numbed herself and dissected the veins in her arm, neck, and groin" so the damage could not be undone. "A lot of people thought it was me."

Sharon at first says nothing that's happened is going to change the way she votes. She's a Democrat who went for Bush, of whom she says, "I never thought he was totally with it to begin with. I got pressure from my husband, who is a down-the-line Republican, and I don't talk about it, or otherwise we have friction." But she also says she feels drawn into civic life in a new way, if only by virtue of the fact that she is still here, in a place where people no longer have the luxury of ignoring one another.

Even more than New Yorkers after 9/11, they have a city to put back together, and the growing suspicion that it is all up to them. While the rest of us carry right on disconnecting—why call when you can e-mail, or talk to the gas station attendant when you can use your credit card at the pump—New Orleanians are moving in the opposite direction. "Two weeks ago, there was a neighborhood party for a candidate for city council, and I went, mostly to reconnect with the neighbors, and I came away fired up."

She goes off to see patients then, but she turns over her office to me and sends in other women to talk to me there, one at a time, starting with a Republican pharmaceutical rep from Mandeville who thinks the government response to Katrina was "probably a little slower than it should have been, but we're stronger, better, safer" for having lived through it. "Kind of like after 9/11."

The next woman Sharon sends in, a patient slathered in

numbing cream, suggests that all the anesthesia in the world could not make her that sanguine: "The federal government let us down the worst, especially when the tape came out showing Bush knew the levees could break." She touches the goop on her face—"I feel kind of funny talking to you with this on"—but then picks right back up and lights right back into the president. "I'm one of the only liberals you'll meet here," she is sure. "My Republican friends, they still defend him." Her mother is such a strong conservative, she says, that "I haven't asked her if she's changed her mind; I'd like to know what she'd say. She's in the waiting room, if you want to talk to her."

What Mom, aka Gail Lemarie, does say is "I have lost a lot of respect for Bush—and had a little bit before this, with the Iraq situation. But the crowning blow was we could get support to the tsunami victims right away, but it was days before they could get it here. And it's been bungled ever since. I am a registered Republican," an early defector from the Democrats in this part of the country, for the Goldwater campaign in '64. But in '08, "I'm not dead-set no matter who is running, and I want to see some finality in Iraq. A good many of my friends are Republicans" from the medical community—her late first husband was a doctor, as are her son and her son-in-law—"and they're definitely disappointed in the Bush administration, from the top down."

Though some of her friends would not vote for a Democrat under any circumstances, she says, "I do think it's going to affect voter turnout in '08. And I am very disappointed that just a few representatives have come to see it. *Shame* on the rest of them! There are some eyes that will not be opened, and some ears that will not hear." She herself is ready to hear a lot more, she says, and invites me to go along with her to a lunchtime talk by Chris Rose, the *Times-Picayune* columnist who has written a book about Katrina, *1 dead in attic*. But I'm already running late for lunch with the Democratic consultant Donna Brazile's oldest sister, Sheryl

McGee, and instead hop in a cab with a driver named Frank, who tells me about his love life and at least pretends to think I'm local. (Another week here and I'd be so southern even my Kentucky cousins couldn't understand me.) "How'd you make it through the storm?" he asks, even now. Because bodies are still being found; it isn't over.

In the courtyard of a tourist joint in the Quarter, Sheryl and I agree that what this town needs is her sister. But in lieu of that, she's looking for inspiration wherever she can find it. She and her new husband watched the movie *Victory at Sea* the night before, and "I thought, 'If Paris can come back, so can we.'" She is a community educator on organ donation and has already remade her life once, after her first husband died in 2001. But one guy who's getting her down at the moment is a fellow Democrat, the mayor: "I can't say I'm a Bush fan, but if I need help from my neighbor, I'm not going to trash him before I get my egg, and we need help. New Orleans is hurting."

When Katrina hit, "I saw people heading to the Superdome, and a sadness came over me. I saw people in line with their babies." She herself made it no farther than a hotel five miles down the road, where "we had to walk down three flights to get water out of the pool to flush the toilet." After that, "I drank for two or three days in Lafayette. My father said, 'Sheryl, this is worse than Korea.' In this post-Katrina world, if you're walking around thinking you don't need help, you don't just have post-traumatic stress; you are a *fool*. But are you going to sit back, or are you going to do something?"

When she finally made it back to the West Bank, across the Mississippi from downtown, "it looked like a bomb had exploded." A church group was already on the scene "from, was it Kentucky or Arkansas? We all suffer from Katrina Brain. It was almost like they were waiting for us to come home, to help us take trees out, and one guy wanted to pray with me. They were like angels, and I couldn't even fix them a sandwich because I didn't have electricity." Now, she guesses, it's over to the people who live here, the real urban pioneers. "Yeah, the levees need to be repaired, and the houses need to be gutted, but if we have the right leadership, we can do this. God provides a way; wherever there's devastation, there's opportunity."

Her cell phone rings, but the sun is out, there's a soft wind in the courtyard, and she lets it go. "That's post-Katrina, too; I don't have to answer every call. I want to live. Katrina, one thing she put on my heart and my mind was to live." Even in the "gruesome" hotel where she was stuck right after the storm, "we all bonded. It was too hot, so we all sat outside and talked about it, and we shared ice and food. Katrina brought out the best and the worst; some people who you thought had it don't. I didn't know what I was like," for that matter, until after her first husband died. "But I found out something inside of me is drawn to hope and doing better."

So did Becky Zaheri, a young doctor's wife who started Katrina Krewe, a volunteer outfit that's cleaning up New Orleans a block at a time. One morning in the Ninth Ward, where I spend a few hours picking up trash with my family and some friends, Becky explains how "you couldn't go back to the old way of life. You couldn't raise kids like this," she says, gesturing toward one of the small mountains of trash we have collected: broken glass, washed-away cutlery, even a toxic teddy bear. "I'm not what you would call a politically inclined person"—when people say this, I notice, they usually mean that they vote Republican but don't want to talk about it—"but I couldn't go back to playing a lot of tennis and exercising. I told my husband that if we were going to raise our kids here, we were going to have to clean up the city, or I was not going to be able to stand it."

Still, for every Becky Zaheri, there seems to be a Gloria Dauphin—a woman who was politically active before the storm but finds herself on hiatus now. Gloria, an executive for the Society for the Prevention of Cruelty to Animals, meets me for a drink after work along with her partner, Cynthia Farin. They've lost their home in the Mid-City section and are living with three cats and two dogs in a trailer in yet another driveway. "Sitting here," in the bar of the Hotel Monteleone, "you can almost forget," Gloria says. It's her first time back in the Quarter.

Before Katrina, she had been organizing a social justice conference based on the poetry of Audre Lorde, Harlem's self-described "black lesbian mother warrior poet." "But since the storm, I can't do anything but work. It's deadened my sense of community action. I used to read the paper all the time, but now" she has a hard time forcing herself to find out what's going on. "I am very angry at the Bush administration, and Clinton, too, let a lot of things fall through the cracks."

"I think the whole city is still in shell shock," says Cynthia, "and Mardi Gras was a huge mistake, because it made everybody think it was okay if we were back to having parties." Gloria went to one of those parties, she says, and it made her sadder than ever, driving through all the empty neighborhoods on the way there. Politically, as they look toward the future, they can think of no Democrat who moves them—not one. Cynthia, who votes for the Green Party when she can, says she's thinking about voting for John McCain. And when you have animal-rights-activist lesbians of color thinking John McCain, do I need to say how far the Democrats still have to go?

Then there are the women here who swear they're better off since Katrina, or that New Orleans is. For instance, my good friend Lori's good friend Susan's mom, Helen Kottemann—I told you this wasn't science—who lives in Metairie. The first thing you notice as you go in Helen's place is the framed *Gone With the Wind* poster in the entryway, and then her doll collection, which includes two Scarletts, one of them in a special glass case in the living room. Susan, who used to run high-end tours in Tanzania—and if she had a bumper sticker might choose something along the lines of I'D RATHER BE IN AFRICA—has already suggested that though she adores her mother, they do not see eye to eye on what is still the elephant in America's living room: race. "I say, 'Mama, I've lived in New York for thirty years and I'm a Democrat now; you can't talk that way around me.'" The way Helen puts it to me is that after all that's happened, "I should hope it will change some things politically; maybe we'll have the first white mayor we've had in years." New Orleans, after all, "is fifty-six percent white now."

Helen, a widow who lived here alone until her son's girlfriend moved in after Katrina, has taken a willfully romantic view of the storm. "The Gulf really reclaimed some places: *Gone With the Wind*," she says, though it no doubt did not seem quite so lyrical when she was trying to get the cat into the box for the last-minute trip to Baton Rouge. "We didn't have local coverage, so we didn't know at first. We just had national and the nut going, 'Look at the wind blowing!' and he's blowing down the street."

At first, Helen claims that all she lost to Katrina was a fence she didn't like anyway—"I was tickled pink"—and later, by her own hand, the magnolia tree in front of her house. She'd planted the tree forty years ago, when Susan was seven years old. "And when I came back, I decided I'd cut it down. I wasn't going to wait for the next storm. It was beautiful, but nothing is that beautiful. I have yet to go into the bad sections—Lakeview, Chalmette—and then you feel guilty because here you sit, high and dry. But the next storm it could be me," she says, stroking her black-and-white cat.

I am not sure whether she's cut down her beautiful tree out of survivor's guilt, or as some kind of offering to the storm, as well as to keep it from crashing into her house in some future gale. But she is determined to show that Katrina didn't get to her in any way that matters. "I'm tired of everybody blaming everybody, like

Bush caused the hurricane to come our way. I'm not one of those naysayers who say the government reneged. *Nobody* anticipated" what happened, she says, though she also says New Orleanians should have known to get out of town. "You'd have to have lived in a damn bubble or in a cave not to have known. Now, thousands of people didn't have a car or were infirm and couldn't get out— one of my sisters-in-law died; she was in a hospital and was taken to a school gym, and that's where her daughter found her. I suspect she wasn't going to live much longer anyway, but you do think they should have been on a generator." That was almost the last thing Helen told me. But wasn't that surely *the* thing?

Another woman who says she's doing better—economically, at least—since the storm is Bridgette Aronson, who has a little restaurant across the bridge on the North Shore in Covington. Business at the Back Porch Grill has tripled post-Katrina, with forty thousand more people suddenly living over there. Bridgette describes herself as "not a chef, just a good southern cook" who, after her divorce, "figured this was the one thing I knew how to do, start cookin'." Even in New Orleans, she found, "they had really good foo-foo food, lots of vertical stuff. But I thought, 'They don't have a good chicken-salad sandwich.'"

Out on the breezy back porch of her place—which had been a bar for sixty years, in a building the previous owner supposedly won in a card game—she says that for her, the human face of the storm is "a woman who worked in my house for twenty-eight years and lived in a subsidized building on Claiborne Avenue" in the city. "She's fine and she's in Atlanta, but she's desperate to come home. She's like family, and I wanted to let her put her FEMA trailer on my property, but, typical New Orleanian, she doesn't want to be over here, and chances are she'll never get to come back. I mean, she *raised* my children—I was there, but I was always working. This is a true loss for me."

Politically? "I'm an American; I don't vote parties at all. I voted for Gore, because I've always thought Bush was a diaper-wearing— I don't trust him. Oh, and Kerry, that's who I voted for" most recently, "even though that wasn't a good choice for me. This is a *very* Republican area—like they wouldn't patronize your business" if you were a known Democrat. She doesn't feel that small-business owners have been so well served by the Republican Party, though, especially since the storm. "The small-business owner really understands how important it is to have a government that works."

Her friend Nanette Schoenewe, who runs the health food grocery down the street, feels that way, too, but is amazed, she says, by how much slack some here are willing to extend to the president still. On the environment, for instance, "I've actually heard people say, 'Oh well, we'll live inside for the rest of our lives.'" Driving back from Nanette's place into the city to see Anne Milling, the Women of the Storm organizer, I listen to Rush Limbaugh on the radio, mocking opponents of the war in Iraq: "Germany and Japan seem to be doing pretty well, and we haven't pulled out of *there* yet." The real question, he says, is when we are going to withdraw from the war on poverty.

Anne, who has a master's degree in modern European history from Yale, has always been a contributor in her community, volunteering with Second Harvesters Food Bank and serving on the boards of the *Times-Picayune* and the New Orleans Museum of Art. "I've always paid attention, but since Katrina, there's been an awakening among women in particular who perhaps didn't read the paper before." The link between environmental protection and storm damage is not new for her, either. Her husband, R. King Milling, was a big oil and gas lawyer before he became president of Whitney National, one of the oldest banks in the South. And he has been trying to tell people for years that preserving the wetlands wasn't about saving the migratory birds and the fish but about protecting the region's economy and investments in coastal areas. Anne is no Cindy Sheehan, in other words, but that's the point. Because when a mover like Anne Milling gets mad, it's harder to write her off as some kind of liberal lunatic.

The first book I notice in Anne's cozy library is Barbara Bush's latest memoir, and I'm guessing that no Democrat would have this volume in plain view when she sets me straight: "We're registered Democrats, but we always vote for the person. King is a banker, and we have a lot of Republican friends. I voted Republican last time, but I would never— The response has just been appalling."

Then she mentions, as so many others have done, one particular African-American face of the storm. In her case, it's "this black man who worked at a Catholic church and cut our grass. In Canada," where she was vacationing when Katrina hit, "I said, 'Oh, who is taking care of Jamal?' For some reason, their phone was working, and I said, 'You have got to get to the Dome!' and I'm yelling, '*Do* it!' And now Jamal says, 'I cannot even tell you what happened'" when he did go to the Superdome, because it was so horrific. Later, when he finally made his way to Houston, "He saw a Whitney Bank there and was smart enough to go in and say, 'Do you know Mr. King?,' and they got him in touch with us.'" Jamal is still in Houston, in Section 8 housing. "And in Washington they have 'Katrina fatigue'? I say, 'You want fatigue, come down here.'"

What was it that Bush did to get Anne's vote? Her response is one I've heard over and over: "It wasn't that Bush was what you wanted," she says slowly. "But where the Democrats failed was with the wrong candidate; they don't seem to get it right. The religious right drives us wild, so it's not that." What about Kerry was so wrong? Big sigh: "We just couldn't vote for him; there was nothing that made us feel he'd do a better job. Little did we know . . ." Even before Katrina, though, she says, she did know that the Bush administration was "slow to support coastal restoration. It always fell on deaf ears, Karl Rove's included, and wasn't a priority. They're so caught up in Iraq, and that's where the dollars are."

And why is protecting the mouth of the Mississippi River not a strategic priority in the homeland? "Because Louisiana has Democrats as leaders," so the Republicans in Congress and the White House would rather rebuild Republican Mississippi, she says without any hesitation. "Because they have Trent Lott and Haley Barbour, they're getting most of the money.[10] And that's annoying, to be polite about it."

10. They did not get most of the money, but more than their share, as Louisianans saw it. In a February '06 story in *The New York Times,* Louisiana officials complained that Congress had shortchanged the state in a $29 billion relief package that gave $5.2 billion housing reconstruction money to Mississippi, which suffered far less damage but has a Republican governor and two GOP senators.

In the Belly of the Bubba

"What makes me mad is I didn't even get taken by some Washington fancy pants; I got taken by a yokel!"

I n some ways, Texas senator Kay Bailey Hutchison is the least of her Democratic challenger's concerns. Because before Barbara Ann Radnofsky can take on her opponent, she has to find a way around her state's press herd. These guys have covered not only the president but Karl Rove, too, see, and are way too savvy to get caught out taking an underfunded no-name (with three names) from that other party even semi-seriously.

So, Barbara Ann sits out in front of a supporter's house on the phone, plowing the same old Astroturf with a columnist for *The Austin American-Statesman*. "We are just going to have to agree to disagree, then," she says into her cell, so many times that at first I think it must be her husband on the line. She rolls her eyes at her aide. Oh: press call. "Gardner," she drawls, "what I mean by 'They couldn't be closer' is that she just hosted a fund-raiser for him. She just defended him in the *Houston Chronicle*. Other Republicans are running away, but Kay Bailey says Tom DeLay is the future. *That's* what I mean by 'they couldn't be closer.' The president hasn't done that. His wife? Who, DeLay's wife? Well, his wife hasn't given him as much money as Kay Bailey, has she?"

She laughs and gets off the phone, shaking her head. "He was determined he was going to get me to say they were in bed together," as if she'd actually been accusing them of trysting somewhere in the basement byways of the Capitol. "He was determined to get me to say that!" A small victory, then? Nah—when W. Gardner Selby's column appears in the paper a couple of days later, what it says is: "Radnofsky says Hutchison's defense of DeLay puts her closer to him than his wife." So on top of being crazy enough to run, she looks plain-old-vanilla crazy, too.

Such is the humbled state of the once great Texas Democratic Party that I have the backseat of their Senate candidate's red Tahoe to myself as she and her one-man "executive campaign committee," Seth Davidson, crisscross the state—stumping, bird-watching, and stopping at funky diners. "I'm the new face of the Democratic Party," she tells me, and herself, I think. But if she isn't, that's too bad, because the Democrats could learn a thing or two from Barbara Ann Radnofsky, whose field operation explains a lot about both her party's situation here and how they might set about improving it. I'm curious to check out the political landscape in Bush's home state, and she is a good guide—and a good candidate, but one with no help at all from her party, left to rub two sticks together if she feels a chill.

Barbara Ann is a forty-nine-year-old Houston lawyer and mediator for Vinson & Elkins, the same place Kay Bailey's husband, Ray Hutchison, does his lawyering. (It's also Attorney General Alberto Gonzales's old firm, though they're even better known for representing Enron and Halliburton.) Until recently, Barbara Ann spent her spare time teaching mediation skills to neurologically challenged kids. But then her anesthesiologist husband took early retirement from M. D. Anderson Cancer Center so she could ride uphill on a shoestring for these last two years, full of purpose and heart and something more: the vital willingness to risk looking foolish.

In her stump speech, she tells how her father's B-17 was shot down over Nazi Germany during World War II, how "flak had pierced his flak jacket, causing his parachute to fail, but as he lay bleeding on the floor of the plane, his bombardier came over and slipped his own parachute on my dad and threw him out of the plane on a line. So I grew up knowing that I am here in this world because of the sacrifice and the risk-taking of those who came before me." In the German POW camp where her father ended up, "the Nazis only came once, and my father only told us about it near the end of his life. He said they came one morning to the Luftkamp, where the prisoners were American and British and Canadian. They asked all the Jews to step forward. And to a man, every one of them stepped forward, saving my father's life. Those men—teenagers, really—stepped forward and saved the world for democracy." Is it so much to ask that we step forward now?

Though she is in no way reticent about criticizing her political adversaries, as a mediator, "common ground is what I'm good at" she says over lunch, en route to an event in Stephenville. At every stop, she speaks about targeting zero abortions, and forgets to eat when she gets going on the topic of calling an end to challenging one another's religious beliefs. Finally, Seth points to her food, and she complies. "Shut up and eat? Okay, okay."

Back on the road, they pass the time by keeping their eyes out for birds. "Sparrow?" she asks. "Meadowlark," he answers. "Turkey vulture?" "Yeah, and a loggerhead shrike." At one point, we turn the car around to get a closer look at an American kestrel, and another time, at a Eurasian collared-dove. Barbara Ann doesn't want to keep the Democratic Women of Erath County waiting, though, so she eventually wrests the binoculars from her driver/manager.

The event is being held in an empty building on the Stephenville town square, where a sign proclaims this THE #1 DAIRY COUNTY IN TEXAS—rich in MOO-LA. As we pull up to the curb, Barbara Ann repeats her host's name under her breath like a mantra, "Marcy Tanter, Marcy Tanter, Marcy Tanter," until a woman wearing a name tag approaches with her hand out: "Hi, Marcy!" Inside, about sixty people are waiting, and Barbara Ann tells them her stories about her dad and asks all the veterans and their families to raise their hands. "My opponent has failed to properly fund veteran affairs," she says. "It's scandalous that there has to be private charity for our retired veterans. The chairwoman on veteran affairs is . . . Kay Bailey Hutchison, who said on the floor of the Senate, 'We need no more money' for them." Barbara Ann is a striking, imposing woman and always wraps up her remarks this way: "So, what's the solution? Oh, I don't know; maybe someone who stands about five foot nine and looks good in purple coats," or whatever it is she's wearing, though the purple does work best.

Another candidate at the Stephenville event, Mary Beth Harrell, who has two sons in the army and is running for Congress, interrupts Barbara Ann's fund-raising pitch to say, "I'll be honest with you; I'd rather have a root canal without anesthetic than ask for money. But the biggest lie since Nazi Germany is that Democrats can't win in this state." Not for the first time, I wonder how so many candidates, including some far more experienced than Mary Beth, managed to miss the memo that comparisons to the Nazis never, ever go anywhere good. Then the county's young party chair, Bill Oxford, Jr., wraps up by inviting everyone to come on over to his house for a State of the Union party that Tuesday, "so we can laugh and hoot and holler." In closing, he asks the crowd to remember one thing about the candidates: "The Democratic Party does not have a whole lot of power right now, so these people are not doing it for the power." [11]

Then the cake is served and checks collected, including a ten-

11. Mary Beth Harrell lost to Republican John R. Carter 38.3 percent to 59.5 percent, and Barbara Ann Radnofsky lost to Kay Bailey Hutchison 35.5 percent to 62.4 percent.

dollar donation to Barbara Ann from a beaming woman who seems delighted to call herself a brand-new Democrat. "I voted for Bush the first time and have always been an Independent, but I'm off the fence now," says Beth Mewhinney, "and for the first time in fifty-nine years, I'm going to vote in the Democratic primary" in the fall. "I've lived here twenty years and didn't even know there were any Democrats here, but I can't say how strongly I'm against all the lives that have been lost" in Iraq. Beth, a crisis counselor for women in abusive relationships, says she has had a hard time watching "one thing after another get taken away from them" as funding for social programs is cut. "It just seems like the Republicans in Washington don't have a heart."

Asked if she knows others here who feel similarly, she has to say no. "I work with some young women, and I try to talk to them, but they are so busy, buying their first homes and so on, and I was like that, too. I'm still not a bumper-sticker kind of person, but I called five people to come here today, and that was a big step for me. I'm trying to get braver. I like for everybody to like me, so it's baby steps."

Milling in the crowd, Barbara Ann is talking immigration to a man with some forceful opinions. He likes the idea of the big fence that the Republicans want to build along the Mexican border, but Barbara Ann does not agree. When Marcy Tanter overhears Barbara Ann saying the unions have sure come around to her point of view, she tries to save the candidate by throwing herself in front of the train, babbling, "Unions in Texas? We have onions, but not unions!" Which Seth decides is as good an exit line as any, and starts urging the candidate toward the door. Turns out, the man Barbara Ann was arguing with had sent her an e-mail asking, "What kind of Jew are you?," and now she's sure glad she sent him a courteous reply. "He took sixty yard signs!" she marvels. She wants Seth, her forty-two-year-old go-to guy, to tell her she smiled enough, which he doesn't. Or that she kept her answers nice and short, but at that, too, he shrugs. He liked what he saw in the crowd, though. "Some of those people were Republicans, just *Republicans*!" he says. "One guy came up with his wife, and I asked if he'd take a sign. He said, 'I can't put your sign in my yard, but I guarantee you've got our vote.'"

On our way to our next stop, we seem to pass more churches than stores still in business; one has a sign that says, WANT A NEW LOOK? HAVE YOUR FAITH LIFTED. A roadside billboard asks, IF YOUR LIFE IS A MOVIE, WHAT IS IT RATED? Then we pass the original Dr Pepper bottling company, which opened here in Dublin, Texas, in 1891. "We gotta stop," Barbara Ann shouts, and jumps out to get her picture taken with a statue of Dr Pepper for her campaign blog. "Pat the peppy part of Dr Pepper!" Seth calls, and she ventures a tap on the doctor's bronze knee. As with any man and woman stuck on the road together for long stretches, there is a certain tension between these two—over his driving and her reaction to it. But they also get silly sometimes, in a way that makes you wonder why so many Democrats still seem to fear above all else getting caught acting like a person, despite the general cry for a president who could double as the dad next door.

At the same time, you wouldn't spend years of your life this way unless you were plenty serious, and Barbara Ann says what she's done is study the traditional Democratic playbook and then try to do the opposite: "All the old hands said, 'There's a model in Texas. You start local, you win a few and lose a few, then after ten years, you move up to state rep. Then after twenty-five years, you try some ladylike statewide office, maybe comptroller, so that in thirty years, you're ready'" to go for a seat in the U.S. Senate. At that rate, she would be camera-ready in her mid-eighties, God willing. "The model hasn't been working. But to do it any other way, I knew I'd have to take three years on the road, because you can't just saunter in off the street, either."

So she started with the six thousand names already in her

Rolodex from years of charitable fund-raising in Houston, and she went to work raising money for others in her party—$150,000 for the redistricted former congressman Nick Lampson in his campaign, which was originally against the old redistricter himself, Tom DeLay—as well as $750,000 so far for her own race. Unlike Mary Beth Harrell, Barbara Ann says she not only doesn't mind dialing for dollars but wouldn't attempt this race otherwise. Scanning today's fund-raising call list kind of pumps her up: "Oh, here's a guy in Sugar Land," where DeLay is from. "He's gonna like me. Oh, and this one has homes in Pawtucket and Southampton; he *needs* to like me." She's also studied polling—other people's polling, because she can't afford her own—and found that "it's an advantage to be a woman; there's a higher level of trust, and voters think women are more committed to good works. Woman against woman is different. But if I were a man, I probably wouldn't have tried it at all."

Just then she spies a flock of birds, dipping and soaring together in a field on the side of the road, and she cries, "So pretty!" Seth sets her straight: "Brown-headed cowbirds. Parasitic nesters. There's been an explosion of them, and it's an ecological catastrophe because they take over the nests of Central American and Mexican migrants, putting pressure on the songbirds and warblers." So, not pretty. Just like the burned-out fields we're passing, and in the distance, another brushfire, another reminder of the drought, and of that other ecological catastrophe that takes some of the fun out of a seventy-degree January day. "We are in Republican country here," Barbara Ann remarks, "but they think disaster management is being poorly handled, too." Disasters that include wildfires as well as hurricanes.

In downtown Abilene, a woman hosting the first fund-raiser of her life is waiting for Barbara Ann in the lobby of the National Center for Children's Illustrated Literature, all flushed in the new red dress she's bought for the occasion. Voters have to get to know

Barbara Ann, who really is a centrist, says the woman, Alice Spier, and they'll start to see that "when Kay Bailey says she's a moderate, she's not that." Another supporter, Becky Haigler, adds that she herself has only recently "seen the light" and become an ex-Republican. "My husband converted in '04, and I came over six months later. I grew up in a very strong Republican family, but they are very quiet now, maybe not ready to say anything but knowing things aren't right. We were *big* Bush supporters when he was governor, and even during the first term." What changed? Her husband was a big supporter of the war in Iraq at first, she says, but the more closely he followed the news in order to refute critics, the more critical he became. "He's got the zeal of the convert now," Becky says.

And her? "I was for small government, and the Bush administration didn't fit that. I was for fiscal responsibility, and they didn't fit that, either. So being pro-life was the last thing, but pro-life is just a party dress Republicans wear, and when we found out that forty-three percent of Democrats are pro-life, too, there went my last reason." Since she made the switch, some people at her church have let her know they're praying for her, or they've remarked, "It's obvious you've lost your faith," so she does feel she's paid a price socially.

The room is bigger than the crowd again tonight, and there is so much food here, a small mountain of mozzarella and tomatoes for the few dozen who've turned out, that every one of them could take home a family-size doggie bag. Two TV stations have sent reporters, but they don't seem to know what to ask—"Why Abilene?" one finally inquires—and both leave before Barbara Ann speaks, thus missing out on a classic "Who's on First?" exchange during the Q and A.

At every stop, Barbara Ann makes an issue of the fence that Kay Bailey and her party want to build along the Mexican border, and she usually gets a few questions on the subject. So when an older man in the audience asks her where she stands on defense, she misunderstands. "It's a mistake, and it won't work," she answers in the snappy, no-fooling way that Seth has been pushing her toward.

Man: "Uh, I didn't understand your answer on defense."
Barbara Ann: "A huge waste."
Man: "You're totally against it?"
Barbara Ann: "I think it's a bad idea, yes."
Man: "So, you think we should cut it *all*?"

Belatedly, after this has gone on for a minute, she bursts out laughing: "Ohhhh, de-*fense*. I thought you said da fence!" Her questioner still looks confused; he sees nothing funny about cutting defense.

I don't hear every question myself, because the guy sitting next to me keeps whispering little asides in my direction. When Barbara Ann asks all the vets to raise their hands, he volunteers that he was a draft dodger, and when she tells how this is her 311th campaign trip, he whistles. "Well, gol-dern." At the mention of Kay Bailey, he wants to know, "Wasn't she a cheerleader?" By the time Barbara Ann finishes, I'm seriously wondering if he wandered in off the street, but then there is Seth, making a beeline for me. "What did he say?" Who? "David, of course! Sitting next to you! He is a *gazillionaire*! No one thought he would even come, and everyone said if he did, he wouldn't say anything because he's too shy! I saw the whole thing, and I think he wants to marry you!" Seth is happy, okay? Because even though turnout was low, the take was high. "I got so many checks in my pocket, I look like I grew a left breast!"

The candidate seems to get more excited about the money she saves, for instance by staying with supporters rather than in hotels. And the woman who puts me up for the night, Robin Burrow, a local Realtor, says she's been well warned against letting it be known that she's a Democrat. "Everyone says it would be bad for business." So when we arrive at a campaign breakfast the next morning, a friend saving a seat for her calls out, "Robin, are you going to be an open Democrat now?"

"Oh yeah, I'm coming out of the closet," she answers. Why now? "Every time this administration needs some money, they look to the most vulnerable," she says. "I think Bush is giving Christians a bad name, and I'm a fundamentalist!" I sit down next to Dora Martinez—"Mama Dora, the Hispanic matriarch," as she's introduced by Dave Haigler, the Democratic convert. "Mexican-Americans were more for the poor people, the needy, when I was young," Dora tells me. "Now I see more young people going over to the Republican Party," including her nephew Jorge Solis, a federal judge in Dallas. Her daughter, though, Anna Martinez Vedro, is president of the Texas Democratic Women's Big Country chapter, the group hosting Barbara Ann this morning. Another woman at our table, Barbara Bachus, asks Anna if she doesn't think Republicans have been losing some ground here lately, because "a lot of them don't love Tom DeLay anymore." Anna's not so sure: "What's most important for us is our Democrats are starting to come out of the closet—the prairie-dog Democrats who were in their hidey holes, afraid it would affect their jobs if anyone knew about their affiliation."

"Because you couldn't be a Christian and be a Democrat," says the woman next to her, Jewell Halford—at least not until the scandals came along. "If you were a Democrat around here, then you just weren't anything." Still, Anna says she isn't banking on DeLay's downfall. "And to be fair, we need to wait for the process to work before we go around saying he's guilty." Barbara Bachus laughs. "Well, that's not any fun." Anna does not join in. "This probably will topple him, but let's let the system work. That's more than they gave us," she says, and sits up very straight. "What

John McCain says about torture is we cannot say we're one kind of country and then torture. Well, this is the same thing. It's about how we want to be treated: fairly." Even at a Democratic event in a part of the country where it requires some courage to let it be known that you're not a Bush fan, the point of moral reference is a Republican, and one who hopes to succeed Bush in '08.

But the biggest problem her party faces here, as Anna sees it, is that so many Hispanics "are just one issue, abortion, which means that on the local level, we need to do more to work on the third part of 'safe, legal, and rare.' We've been neglecting the 'rare.'" Bah, Jewell says: "Everyone's against abortion until your thirteen-year-old comes up pregnant." Barbara Bachus thinks Democrats have gotten too intimidated to talk about social issues at all anymore. "We're scared, and the far right has made us this way." Nooo, Anna answers. "Losing elections has made us this way." Barbara Bachus says what she is pining for is a candidate who "would get up there and tell us what they really feel"—the true F-word for Democrats, who seem to have lost all confidence in themselves while trying to behave like slightly more reasonable Republicans. "They're good and decent, but they're frightened."

After the huevos rancheros and melon, the Senate candidate rises to speak, but she does not go with the stump speech today. This morning's headlines, she says, have supplied her with another example of why Republicans, too, should be fed up by now. Exxon has reported a record $17 billion profit for the year, and over $5 billion in the last quarter alone—a record for any company, in any year, in part from upping their profit margin after Hurricane Katrina. "Thank goodness we gave them that tax incentive" for drilling. But she's so moved, she says, when she sees people here stepping forward to make things right. "Look, stepping forward as a Democrat in Texas is not the same thing, of course, as those men in World War Two who stepped forward and saved my father's life. But it isn't always easy to step forward. And Robin, you are doing the right thing."

Robin is not easy with the praise. "It occurs to me," she says, "that one of the things that will defeat the Democrats is the Democrats; they're discouraged and depressed." Roger Spier, Alice's husband, who is a retired surgeon and one of the handful of men in the room, says, "There's a fear of being identified, and a defeatist attitude. We're pretty isolated out here," he says, like this is East Germany and it's 1960. "Where is it different?" Well, in Lubbock, Barbara Ann says, she was invited to give the Veterans Day address at the VFW, and isn't there hope in that?

Dave Haigler, whose bolo tie is held in place with a little gold ornament—oh, in the shape of a handgun—interrupts her to demand a more convincing sign of life in his new party. "Look, people think you're crazy to take on such an uphill battle, and they look at us and say we're crazy for thinking it can work. So tell us the secret to how we can get more people involved and"—here he slams his fist on the table—"get the passion!"

Barbara Ann mulls this for a minute. "Alice, had you ever done a fund-raiser before last night?"

"No," Alice responds. "And every vote counts in this election; it's not like the presidential." Sadly, at this everyone nods. Her husband says he's already pretty alert to any opportunity to proselytize. "Everybody knows I have a big mouth, and I've made a point of talking to people in grocery lines and generally being obnoxious around town. You get a few sourpusses, but you don't care about those people anyway, and you'd be surprised at the response. I keep bumper stickers in my car and give them out." While he's telling all this, the candidate is pacing, impatient to get back on point, which is the money she'll need to run a real race. She cannot resist noting that her opponent has spent $900,000 campaigning in the first three quarters of the year, though she doesn't even have a primary. "And what did she spend that money on?" she wonders.

"Makeup?" offers Roger. "Botox?"

"Oh, Tammy Faye Hutchison?" another man in the crowd shouts out.

"Gentlemen, gentlemen," Barbara Ann says; she does not have time for such swipes. What she really needs, she says out loud, is some national media exposure, "a level playing field," and maybe even the chance to mix it up with Bill O'Reilly. "You'll never have that with Bill O'Reilly," Roger cracks, "unless you bring a loofah."

For now, anyway, Barbara Ann is just glad to have been able to snag meetings with local editorial boards. She arrives over an hour early for her appointment at the *Fort Worth Star-Telegram*, where she ends up working her way through all the miniature Hershey Krackles in the waiting room candy dish before they finally call her in. You never know what these interviews are going to turn on, and Barbara Ann ends up spending an inordinate amount of time in this one sparring with the editorial page editor, Paul Harral, over whether perjury is or is not a serious offense—only to learn, at the end of the meeting, that a buddy of his was once charged with that crime.

What the deputy editorial page editor, Jill Labbe, objects to is Barbara Ann's characterization of a proposal that would put peace officers on patrol for illegal immigrants as "Barney Fife at the border." (I feel compelled to note that this was before Don Knotts died.) Uh-oh, yes, Jill's husband is a peace officer, as it turns out, and she observes that those officers have to go through rather rigorous training, actually. When we chat after the meeting, Jill, who goes by the nickname J.R., does not hesitate to characterize herself as "a Republican going Democrat." "I am sickened by my party," she tells me—for one thing, over the domestic spying that she feels sure must have included surveillance of her e-mails to her husband, who spent the last two years as a soldier in Afghanistan. "When he came home, he said, 'You realize we've been monitored.' What everybody says is, 'If you're not doing anything wrong, it shouldn't bother you.' But I'm not doing anything wrong, and it pisses me off! Today it's some guy you don't know named Akmed, and tomorrow it's your next-door neighbor."

Still, candidates like Barbara Ann have a long way to go to take advantage of the Texas-size opening they have with disillusioned Republican women like J.R. Her party's structure is so weakened that she has to spend much of her time and money reinventing the wheel, and with next to no help from the national party, she's left building one of those famous bridges to nowhere. The last day I'm with Barbara Ann, she fires one aide for spending too much on a fund-raiser and rids herself of a second neophyte consultant—the only kind she could afford—who did not live up to expectations, either. Seth tries to get her to look at the bright side: Hey, she paid the consultant only $1,700, a pittance next to the millions national Democrats have wasted on various masterminds. "Oh, I know," she says, "but what makes me mad is I didn't even get taken by some Washington fancy pants; I got taken by a yokel!"

Then she and Seth are off for Galveston, and I stay on with friends in Dallas, where I worked for six years at my first reporting job, at *The Dallas Morning News*. It occurs to me that Barbara Ann might have reminded her supporters in Abilene, so desperate for signs of a few pink streaks on the horizon, that even Dallas County almost went Democratic in '04—and, in the category of "All Things Are Possible for $800," elected its first Hispanic lesbian sheriff. "I had a novice team that had never been told 'You can't do that,'" explains Sheriff Lupe Valdez. "I had nothing but new people who were hungry and believed in me, and I was running against a good old boy who was part of the situation"—which involved multiple allegations of corruption. "You cannot imagine the shape the department is in; I've had to start over from scratch. But now, everywhere I go, I meet Republicans who do one of these," she says, covering her mouth and whispering furtively, "'I voted for you.'"

Bush, who lived here when he owned the Texas Rangers, edged Kerry out by fewer than ten thousand votes, taking Dallas County with only 50 percent to Kerry's 49. Which is especially interesting because even more than Houston or Midland, I've always thought, Dallas has so much in common with W. that to understand the one is to get the other, too. Dallas is all business, and its Republicans not particularly socially conservative (see Valdez, Lupe). When the wedge issues don't play, Democrats have a chance, even on their opponents' home turf.[12]

Yet the media, I'm sorry to say, does not offer Barbara anything resembling a fair hearing. When reporters do speak with her, their only real question is some variation on: "What are you, nuts?" Several of my old friends in journalism here even seem anxious for me when I tell them I've been traveling with her: "You do know she's going to lose, right?" They mean this kindly; they wouldn't want me to embarrass myself by wasting my time listening to someone who is not a winner.

On one of my last nights in town, I attend a party that a stockbroker friend of mine is having at an upscale wine bar in Oak Lawn, where she is schmoozing for business and I for opinions. It's there that I see most clearly all that the Democrats are up against, even when the social issues are off the table. This is a city where women wear full makeup on late-night ice cream runs to the Tom Thumb, and the mostly female crowd is so soigné that I can't help but recall my own subpar efforts in this regard—as when I wore a pair of three-inch turquoise heels to work as a baby cop reporter and then got that sinking feeling, literally, as they melted into the asphalt at a midsummer's crime scene near Love Field.

12. According to the November 22, 2006 *Dallas Voice,* the gay and lesbian newspaper, Dallas is now on a par with New York and Los Angels in its number of openly gay public officials. On November 7, voters elected an openly gay county judge, Jim Foster, and an openly gay district clerk, Gary Fitzsimmons. They join Sheriff Valdez and Constable Mike Dupree.

Among these professional women in their twenties, thirties, and forties, abortion isn't mentioned once all night; they are outraged opponents of social programs and say things like "I'm such a Republican because I believe in hard work, and Democrats believe in handouts." And, "the last time I voted for a Democrat was for Ann Richards, and I'm still paying for that; now we're subsidizing the schools in Laredo." And, "These Katrina people don't want to work; they watch TV all day, and they don't take care of anything, but you still have to rent to them. I feel sorry for them, but this has put them right at our doorstep." These women are beside the point for even moderate Democrats like Barbara Ann, because they cannot be moved. Yet theirs are the most difficult voices for me to listen to, because they so challenge my whole "We Are the World" notion of sisterhood; I hear Katrina victims called lazy and can feel the muscles under my scapulae tightening.

Though I say I respect all points of view, that clearly isn't true, and soon after my Texas trip, I hear the voice of my conscience in an op-ed in *The New York Times* under the headline OUR FAITH IN LETTING IT ALL HANG OUT. Its author, the literary theorist Stanley Fish, suggests that respect is often just condescension by other means: "The first tenet of the liberal religion is that everything (at least in the realm of expression and ideas) is to be permitted, but nothing is to be taken seriously. . . . The thing about respect is that it doesn't cost you anything; its generosity is barely skin-deep and is in fact a form of condescension: I respect you; now don't bother me." There's something to that. But is Fish's argument another excuse for incivility?

Dallas is where I met my husband, and where we began our ongoing argument about southern manners. He finds them phony and insulting, while I in all cases much prefer insincere courtesy to heartfelt rudeness; it's called civilization. And while women may bring more emotion than men do to choices, political and otherwise, the place feeling leads us can be difficult to predict. Unaccountably, for instance, the woman at the wine bar who argued most vociferously against "handouts" is also the one I found most disarming. Near the end of the evening, she took a deep breath and said, "I feel like a snooty bitch after saying all that, but I think it's because I have a sister who is a loser, a taker, and her way out is to go for bankruptcy and not even try. When I was out of work, I worked temp jobs; when she was laid off, she took WIC and all the subsidies, but she still has the cell phone and the satellite dish. That's what's made me anti–social programs. It would be different if I saw her making an effort." A liberal rationale if ever I heard one, and I'm a sucker for it. But then, understanding is not agreeing, and real respect does *not* mean we can all get along. As Fish suggests, it might mean the opposite.

Border Wars

*"If the general public knew the stories of the
people we work with, it would resonate,
and they'd say, 'That could be me.'"*

I am in my car before dawn, having what the radio DJ is calling
"a musical martini" eye-opener of Diana Krall and Dean Martin
as I watch the Sonoran Desert wake up. I've come out here to
listen to women on the front lines of the immigration debate, but
I also want to get a better sense of the people they're arguing over,
the people who risk their lives crossing this desert. More than two
thousand of them have died trying since 1998, according to the
inter-faith humanitarian group No More Deaths. So I am driving
out to meet Victoria Lopez, a young lawyer who represents the undocumented, at the Florence Detention Center, where they are
held before being sent back to Mexico.

Florence is midway between Phoenix and Tucson, an Old
West mining town staked out in 1866, with a haphazard feel to it,
somehow—a place that, according to the town website, was
"named for someone's sister or daughter." Though I have gotten
careful directions from Victoria, I can see why she seemed to feel I
couldn't go wrong: There is nothing else out here for many miles
around. The closest hospital is twenty-six miles away, past the
monument to the movie cowboy Tom Mix, who died just outside

town in a car crash in 1940. About a thousand migrant detainees are held in Florence, in a flat box of a prison surrounded by a high fence topped off with barbed wire—an enterprise that is the major employer, along with the Arizona state prison. Detention is what the town of Florence does.

Victoria is a slender woman from Chicago, a thirty-year-old Penn Law grad who came to the Florence Immigrant and Refugee Rights Project on an internship and fell in love with the work; she has been here five years and put down roots. We have to leave our purses with the female guard at the gate before we're allowed in, and it takes some doing to persuade the guard to let me in with a notebook and pen. Victoria carries nothing.

I guess I have smuggled in a few biases with me, too, because I am a little surprised to see that Victoria is on completely collegial terms with the guards inside; she treats them with deference, and they return the respect. She makes their lives easier, too, making sure the detainees have access to counsel.

The first thing the guards rush to tell her after we are buzzed in is that half of the guys who were supposed to be in court first thing this morning won't be there after all, because there was some mix-up and they were not given the necessary medical clearance. Soon we are escorted to the courtroom, where several rows of detainees in prison jumpsuits and plastic ID bracelets are waiting. There is only one woman detainee, and she has been seated separately, nearer the judge's bench. Victoria approaches her first, but the woman, who is painfully thin, seems too afraid to speak; she is sitting with her hands tucked between her legs, and when Victoria explains in Spanish what's going to happen this morning, she only nods.

Victoria stands before all of the detainees then, and slowly explains that she is not from the police and is not employed by the courts; she is an independent lawyer whose services are free. She has a nice way about her, at once correct and approachable. Later, each of the detainees will be asked if he wants to be deported right away—a bus to Nogales leaves here every night—or if he prefers to stay on and speak with Victoria about any information that might provide grounds for an appeal. "Is there anyone who was born here?" she asks the group. No hands go up. "Anyone have a green card? Or family members who have papers?" Not immediate family, though everyone seems to have someone—an uncle, aunt, or cousin. One man wants to know whether you get sent back to Mexico or kept in jail here if you have a felony on your record, even if, just for example, you have also been a student and done years of honest work. This last phrase—*trabajo honesto*—he keeps repeating. Victoria answers that it depends on the felony, and that she will be glad to speak to him about it privately.

A second man has no question that I can tell, but he explains that he has a pregnant wife and children in Mexico with no way to support them. A third says he was deported five years ago after a DUI; can they keep him out permanently because of that? Yet another seems on the verge of tears as he tells about how he came from Guatemala "to work and better my life, that's all." Then a man with one eye swollen shut rubs his hands together and says he personally cannot wait to get back to Mexico: "*Adelante!*" he calls, and the others smile for the first time. "I want to go home, man," he adds in English. In the end, only the woman, an asylum seeker from Colombia, wants to stay and meet with Victoria later. "Another time, then," Victoria says to the others in Spanish.

One by one, they are sent next door to the courtroom where the formal deportment hearings are held. There, Judge Scott M. Jeffries explains to each man, "The Department of Homeland Security has placed you in removal hearings because they say you are not a citizen. The purpose of this hearing is to see whether the allegations are true. You have a right to an attorney; would you like more time to talk to an attorney?"

Once under way, individual hearings are brief. Each detainee, wearing earphones that provide simultaneous translation into Spanish, is asked if he is a citizen or if either of his parents is a citizen, if he came into the country illegally, and if there is any reason he is afraid to go back. No, the first man says. Has he been deported before? Yes. "I order you deported, sir." After all of the horror stories out of Abu Ghraib and Gitmo, the dull ritual of due process unexpectedly fills me with the pride I guess we're prone to.

Victoria, on the other hand, is shaken, despite having seen it all so many times before. "Every time I go, I find it jarring; it throws me slightly off," she says as we walk out. Back in her office, in a small adobe building a mile up the road, she shows me how one of her legal colleagues—all ten of her coworkers are women—has moved her desk so that instead of seeing only the unbroken desertscape out of her window, she can stare directly at the ugliness of the detention center where her clients live. "Hardcore," Victoria says, shaking her head.

When she was here as an intern, "I remember calling home sobbing and telling my dad I was working with this Pakistani man with three daughters, just like my dad has—he showed me pictures of them—and I will never forget saying, 'He is just like you.'" Her dad came to this country from Ecuador at age ten, and her mother is second-generation Greek-American. As Victoria was growing up in Chicago's Lincoln Park neighborhood, "my political awareness came from the stories of my father growing up and feeling ostracized by kids, or the teacher would get really upset with him when he'd slip back into Spanish. That shaped the way I think about what's fair." Still, after her five years here, she says, "You have to be outraged to do this work, and it's hard to sustain." Which is why her colleague prefers to keep the prison right in her face.

What Victoria doesn't get about the whole political debate, she says, is how little account it takes of the situation of the immigrants themselves: "People always say, 'They need to find a legal way,' but there are so few ways to come here legally. When you say, 'Why did you come here?,' people say, 'I had to do something. I want to send my kids to school, and I couldn't just sell fruit on the side of the road.'" Though it is widely believed that undocumented immigrants qualify for all sorts of benevolence in this country, "you *don't* get benefits, and in most cases, you don't qualify for health insurance. In Arizona, you can't even get a driver's license." (In fact, according to the nonpartisan Center for Immigration Studies, only 6 percent of immigrants receive food stamps, one of the easiest government aid programs to qualify for.) "The entire discussion is misframed and driven by racism," Victoria thinks, though she also feels sure that "if the general public knew the stories of the people we work with, it would resonate, and they'd say, 'That could be me.'"

The detention center here is "much better" than the ones in Texas and New Jersey, she says, "where folks are strip-searched." Two judges who work at the center in Florence even came to her office last week "and said, 'What can we be doing better?' There is a level of respect for our role." The national debate scares her, though: "It's amazing the work people are doing to get the word out and organize the wonderful marches" in support of immigrants, "but I don't know what's next. Clearly, minds have been made up" in Washington, where immigration reform proposals being batted around include everything from an expanded guest worker program to making it a felony to so much as offer an immigrant aid. As long as it remains unclear which way the legislation will go, "that's frightening," Victoria says. "We talk all the time about what this is going to mean for us. Will we see more people in the detention center? That's frightening for us," she repeats. All the more so because, like abortion, illegal immigration cannot be legislated away so easily.

Still, some common sense could ease pressure on both sides of the debate. "They should be picking and choosing who we're actually detaining. I have no fantasy that we're going to shut them down," she says of the detention centers. "In the real world, not Victoria's world, there will always be those. But we need to understand who is being detained and at what cost."

I am due back in town, but I can't tear myself away before prying a bit, just to keep my skills up, and when I ask about her husband, Victoria grins and says, "Are you ready for this? He's an immigration agent, born and raised in the town of Florence." Actually, it seems perfect. I wonder what the woman I'm meeting for lunch, in another universe, at a mall back in Scottsdale—"the Beverly Hills of the desert," *The New York Times* once called it—would think about Victoria and her husband. My lunch date, Alena Lyras Simcox, is married to Chris Simcox, the president of the Minuteman Civil Defense Corps, a self-appointed border watch group that even George W. Bush once referred to as a bunch of "vigilantes." There is a separate Minutewoman Project, which referred me to Alena, the twenty-six-year-old first lady of the Minutemen. About ten seconds after meeting her, though, I am forced to let go of the idea that I already know what the Minutepeople are about—or this particular one, anyway.

Pregnant, huffing from the hurry and running even later than I typically do, Alena arrives with her four-year-old son and launches without any delay into her story, which as she tells it, begins on 9/11. She was living on the Upper East Side and was four months pregnant by a boyfriend she describes as "someone from Mexico. And we were on Long Island on vacation, en route back to the city. We stopped at a local vegetable stand I've been going to since I was three, and I saw the first building collapse on their TV. So we immediately got food and went back to our place in the Hamptons." (Now you're thinking Martha Stewart and Donna Karan, kiss-kiss and where's the chardonnay? Don't.)

Alena's grandfather was NYPD, one uncle was NYFD, and another uncle worked for the Port Authority. Years ago, her mother and father both worked in Tower One, in an insurance office on the thirty-first floor, "and my uncle's a bus driver who had just dropped people off at the World Trade Center and went back and put bodies on the bus." In the aftermath of the tragedy, "we were going to three and four funerals a day, out of respect. I was pregnant but we"—Alena and her mom—"felt like it was our duty." With no bodies to bury, "they were burying their hats, swords, and guns. One buried a vial of blood, and that was tough to see." Since then, Alena and her mother have been working on a book about the victims of 9/11. "I'm a videographer, and my mother said, 'You can help,'" so she's been taping interviews with survivors.

The more Alena talks, the harder I find it to keep track of her story. She says she grew up "bicoastally" in California and New York, but then she says she grew up in Phoenix. And she is preoccupied with 9/11 in a way that is discomfiting: "I had a chance to hear the voices from the 911 tapes, and I heard it before everyone else heard it, and in November, we got permission to go up on the family viewing deck" at Ground Zero. "I ended up signing my name right next to the president's. I took my mask off and smelled dead bodies. Have you ever smelled a dead body? It's like a deer— a sweet, salty, burning kind of smell. Suzanne Somers was standing next to me, and she went, 'Ugh.'" Alena's son, attending to his grilled cheese, doesn't react to any of this.

Some of her narrative just doesn't track, to the point that I'm not sure what to believe. What is clearly the truth, though, is that for Alena, the immigration issue has nothing to do with racism and everything to do with security and her lack of it. After 9/11, "I did not feel safe" in New York. "What's to keep someone from putting a bomb on the train I'm on? And they hardly even check the tankers, and at Kennedy, I found a bag unattended. I can't enjoy my life anymore. I might be a little bit hypochondriac, but I'd rather have my son right next to me."

"Mommy, I *am* right next to you," her little boy says, laughing. The two of them and her mom came to Phoenix on vacation a little over a year ago, with the idea of looking around for a house. Right around that time, "I got an e-mail from someone saying, 'Check out this Minuteman Project,' and I just thought the name was great, because I'm from Boston." Boston? I thought you said California and New York and Phoenix? Well, Boston for college, she amends. She met Chris Simcox soon afterward, and became his third wife several months later. "The illegals are not really the issue—if I was one of them, I'd want to come here myself, and they work hard—it's about closing the border," she says. "The day after 9/11, the president came on TV and said, 'We need you to be vigilant,' and basically, that's what we live by." As far as the political debate goes, Alena is way moderate by Minuteman standards, she says, because most of them are mad as hell at the president, and she is not: "I voted for Bush twice and would never say anything bad about him." But at the mention of the president, her son shouts, "I hate him!" "No, you don't," she says, and looks mortified.

Oh, I know a lot of people who feel that way, I assure her. "I do, too," she says. "And I *don't* agree with him not securing the borders. What's stopping those people from carrying a nuclear bomb across? Yet we send troops to secure other borders. If I were the president, I wouldn't have gone to Iraq. I would have secured the borders here. They didn't bomb Iraq, they bombed us here." I certainly do agree with her that "homeland security" is nothing but a phrase, and one with overtones I'd rather not cozy up to.

It's because the borders are not secure, Alena insists, that the Minutemen are out there watching. "You sit on the border and see people coming across at night, fifteen or fifty people at a time, and it's frightening." It's *frightening,* she repeats, just as Victoria Lopez had earlier. I ask Alena why, if it's so scary, she would want to spend whole nights sitting out in the desert in the dark. She answers by telling me how she realized she was going to marry her husband on their first night out together on patrol: "I had had numerous amounts of people ask me if I wanted to go out with them"—out to keep watch on the border—"and I said no. But when he asked, I said yes."

All you do, she explains, is keep a lookout and call Border Patrol on your cell when you see something, and they're there within five or ten minutes. But "it's dark out there, and with the anticipation of waiting in the desert in the middle of the night, it's like if they see you, what's going to stop them from shooting at you? You're putting your life on the line, and it's like being a policeman, kind of. I've never trusted anybody like I trusted" Chris Simcox. Before that, "I was all alone."

Her son corrects her: "No, you weren't. You were hanging out with Grandma and me." If I were staying over the weekend, she says, I could go out with them to help put up the private fence they're building on the border, "modeled after the Israeli fences that were very effective. Lock the gates," she says, nodding, no malice and all fear. "Don't let anybody in." I can't help thinking that a more humane immigration policy might actually ease some of Alena's anxiety, because it would separate the Mexican candy vendors from the terrorists.

Later that afternoon, I am supposed to meet a young woman from the pro-immigrant group Inmigrantes Sin Fronteras (Immigrants Without Borders) in Barrios Unidos Park downtown, where they're getting together to plan a celebration to mark their one-year anniversary. It's this grassroots, up-from-nowhere organization that the local papers say was largely responsible for turning out four thousand people at a demonstration in front of the state capital back in January, and an unheard-of twenty thousand in March, when the *East Valley Tribune* reported that "marchers filled a solid mile along North 24th Street." *The Arizona Republic* has described the group as "a powerful new organization . . . that some say is helping shape the debate in Arizona over illegal immigration." On the drive over, I think about the way the Inmigrantes are taking matters into their own hands, and in doing so have more in common with the Minutemen and -women than either group might like to think.

The first woman I meet at the park turns out to be the last, because we keep talking while the sun sets and then some, until it is so dark I cannot see my notebook anymore. Luz Aguilar is a forty-nine-year-old housekeeper who says that until this movement came along, she, too, had been living fearfully. She cries still when she talks about psychic wounds that go back to her childhood in Mexico. But getting involved politically, she says, has given her a whole new lease on everything.

She started by listening to *Vamos a Platicar,* or Let's Talk, on KIDR-AM (740), the talk show hosted by Elías Bermúdez that went on the air in May 2005 and gave birth to their movement. These days, Luz is such a frequent radio caller that "her voice is very well known," her young friend Nadia Meza says, bragging on Luz's behalf. Luz is an old-school kind of girl who can't help lecturing the younger generation about personal responsibility: "I don't want people to think we're criminals and drug dealers. That is *not* what we are, and I'm fine if they kick those people out." One of her subthemes is how out of place the Mexican flag is here: "We are in a country that is not ours, and we have to show respect. So hold your Mexican flag in your heart, but it's the American anthem we have to learn. We have to have the right attitude and the right message, and respect the American laws."

Luz is president of the East Phoenix chapter of the Inmigrantes Sin Fronteras, and "it's beautiful when we're together. It's so positive it helps me with my traumas." After seventeen years in the country, she is learning English for the first time, at a local women's center, though she is still too timid to try any on me. It's especially difficult, she says, because her hearing was impaired as a result of all the times her ears were boxed as a kid. But lately, "I have learned I don't have to carry guilt that isn't mine. I say no more now, and am fearful less"—though not fearless, no. I see that political involvement as a road to self-actualization is becoming a theme here, and one I in no way wish to belittle. To change anything at all in our world, we do have to believe ourselves and others capable of change. Otherwise, there is no lock anywhere strong enough to make us feel safe.

What Luz left behind in Mexico was a husband who drank and a job in a Coca-Cola bottling company that paid thirty dollars a week. When she crossed the border in 1989, "I walked, and back then there was no security, and it wasn't hard." She is on the path to citizenship now and reflexively makes her case to me: "I've never had a traffic ticket; I contribute. I can see that my boss values me, and she makes me feel like a friend, not a servant or a criminal. People value me now; I spoke on the radio yesterday, and a woman called in and said, 'I love to listen to you, you make me see that I matter, as a mother, as a worker, and as a woman.'"

A little wind is kicking up at the end of an airless afternoon, and blowing sand on us as the light fades. "I don't go to church," Luz says as she tries to brush some of the dust out of her short red hair, "but I believe in God more than ever, and I believe in immigrant reform." By the time it is dark, we are covered in the grit that blew in at sunset, and for some reason, as giddy as if we'd been into the tequila. "We will triumph" politically in the end, Luz says, laughing. "But I feel like we already have."

The previous afternoon, a handful of women from local evangelical churches, dressed up in suits and heels as if on their way to services, had staked out front-row seats in the capital for a scheduled hearing on HB2577, a bill that would have local police rounding up undocumented immigrants under Arizona's trespassing laws. As the Republican chairman of the conference committee, State Representative Russell Pearce, got started, one of these women leaned over and filled me in on the players. "The one talking right now is the devil," she whispered. Pearce is a former deputy sheriff in Maricopa County, and he never even looked up when Representative Ben Miranda, a Democrat and the only Hispanic member of the committee, asked if anybody had considered the constitutionality of the thing. "We were very careful," Pearce answered, still looking down through glasses more than halfway down his nose. The Republican majority then approved the Pearce Amendment; hearing adjourned.

"Can I at least make a statement on the record?" Miranda asked while his fellow lawmakers rustled papers, signaling their intention to exit sooner rather than later.

"We're adjourned," Pearce said. "If I had known—"

"Mr. Chair, you have ample power to reopen the hearing."

"We are adjourned."

This went on until State Senator Barbara Leff, the Republican who had sponsored the Senate version of the bill, said wearily, "Okay, Mr. Miranda, out of the goodness of my heart—" and he raced into his opening: "I don't think there's any improvement we could make that would pass constitutional muster, and we're passing an unfunded mandate. If we allow trespassing to be used as a basis for detaining them, the result will be billions of dollars, and there's no way you're going to train police officers to be immigration officers. And the children, to deny them access to university is unconscionable. And employer sanctions I'm against, because you can bet your bottom dollar they're not going to be against the Marriotts and the Denny's. I did thirteen months in Vietnam, and I can tell you, we never closed that country from the outside."

Pearce looked to have been doodling through all of this, but Miranda thanked him after he wrapped up. "Actually, you can thank *Madam* Chairman," Barbara Leff said, correcting him, "because *I'm* the one who gave you the time." Spend five minutes around lawmakers, and you'd swear you were back on the pre-school playground, not much caring who started it and repeatedly calling, "Work it out!" But this is a level of disrespect my grandmother would have called "beyond the beyonds."

On her way out of the hearing room, Magdalena Schwartz, a copastor, with her sister and brother-in-law, of the Iglesia Palabra de Vida in Mesa, said, "Do you see how he [Pearce] talks with hate?"

"And that was the nicest one I've been to," said her friend Linda Herrera, "because there were cameras."

More and more frequently now, there are cameras, and that's because people like Magdalena are turning out those record crowds for marches protesting proposals such as the bill theoretically under discussion here. Vice president of the Inmigrantes Sin Fronteras, Magdalena views the debate through an unambiguously partisan prism: "Republicans here control the state, and it's like, 'This is *our* land; you don't have any right to live here.'" Though Russell Pearce may or may not know it yet, Magdalena Schwartz is the future—and not only on this issue. For the Democratic Party, turned-on new Hispanic voters like her—and from an evangelical church!—are what hope looks like.

Nadia was with Magdalena, talking about how close she'd come to getting fired from her job as a paralegal over all the time she's been spending as a volunteer for the group. "I don't know much about politics," she said, "but persistence is more important. I was a passive citizen, just a regular citizen walking around and doing nothing for the community, then I started listening to the radio." A male friend who passed Nadia and the others on his way out of the capital as she was saying this called out jokingly, "You women are getting too assertive, almost *aggressive*," and Nadia pocketed the compliment. "When we have women's meetings," she said, "the energy flows."

The energy flows pretty easily on both sides of this issue, of course, which is what makes the politics of immigration so tricky, and why George W. Bush has been working overtime to keep his balance on his float in this particular parade—now throwing a shiny bauble to the anti-immigrant crowd on one side, and then a little something to the Hispanic community, the *growing* Hispanic community, on the other. In the long run, no party can afford to alienate Hispanic voters, many of whom are culturally conservative and as gettable for the Republicans as for the Democrats. So far, Linda has to admit, "the legislation in the state isn't going too good, but our unity is." [13] They are in this for the long pull, Magdalena says. She compares their struggle to that of Martin Luther King, Jr., then adds that their more immediate role model is Chile's first woman president, Michelle Bachelet, "whose papa was killed by Pinochet. I am *so* proud," she says, and not only of Bachelet.

13. Ultimately, the only national immigration legislation Congress passed this year authorizes spending $1.2 billion for a seven-hundred-mile fence along a portion of our country's two-thousand-mile border with Mexico. In Arizona, Democratic Governor Janet Napolitano vetoed bills that would have barred undocumented immigrants from attending adult ed classes and given state and local police the power to enforce immigration laws. But she did sign into law a bill that bars local governments from putting taxpayer dollars into day labor centers that help undocumented workers find jobs. The Inmigrantes Sin Fronteras remain active, and the last time Luz Aguilar called me, she was speaking English.

Disparate Housewives

"I vote like a Democrat, but I mother like a Republican."

There are swing voters and then there is Beth Barach, who swung all the way from Ralph Nader in 2000 to George W. Bush in '04. One of those deadly exurban WMW (white married women) whose defection has been hard on the Democratic Party, Beth grew up helping her mom, a stalwart of the League of Women Voters, campaign door-to-door for local candidates in Westchester County, north of New York City. "I've always been a registered Democrat," she says, "but I'm not a bleeding-heart liberal like my mom is. I have an MBA, and I'm more of a businesswoman."

Beth has done well, in other words, and feels she has outgrown her political roots. Yet she insists that her shift to the right is as much about popular culture as it is about fiscal policy. "I'm very conservative on a lot of the social issues," she says. That's even though she is strongly pro-choice. Even though, as she puts it, "being Jewish, I always have concerns about the Christian mindset creeping in" to the Republican Party. And even though she feels reassured, she says, that there is an outfit like the Log Cabin Republicans, the party's gay and lesbian organization—because if they don't have a problem with the GOP, why should she?

Most of us would glance over this collection of views and peg Beth as a social liberal. But when she says she is conservative on social issues, what she means is that she doesn't necessarily want to be too closely associated with the word "liberal." What she means is that she identifies terrible television and general bad behavior with the party she grew up in. Beth has one child when we meet, and he's two. So she's speaking figuratively when she explains her new political leanings this way: "I don't want my twelve-year-old having oral sex with five guys in school on a dare! I'm in lots of moms' groups, and a lot of us feel there should be less sexualization of kids. A lot of us feel 'Let's err on the conservative side,' and we associate that with politics. We feel like Democrats are so out of date, with their socialist, sixties-esque ideas; they haven't evolved, and they don't speak to me."

It isn't only in the Heartland, in other words, but even here in blue, blue Massachusetts, that the loosening of standards gets tagged as a Democratic phenomenon. That is hardly a new argument; Woodstock seems to be forever linked to Democrats who are ready for retirement now, and Bill Clinton might as well have invented nookie for all the credit he gets for popularizing it.

But during an evening with Beth and some friends from one of her moms' groups, I am a bit surprised to see that the Democrats are losing highly educated northeastern women in their thirties—women the party counts on—over this perception. What's more, even the Democrats among them seem to associate Republican leanings not only with material success but with parental success, with basic responsible parenting. And even those who are pro-choice, like Beth, have come to see the "social conservatism" label as a kind of moral status symbol.

Beth and her husband, a real estate developer, are still settling into their dream house on a wooded country lane, thirty miles west of Boston. Before their son was born, Beth was a marketing manager in the high-tech industry, and she is equally proud of her résumé and of her decision to file it away for now. While she feels isolated out here at times, she reads widely and subscribes to two daily newspapers, *The Wall Street Journal* and *The Boston Globe.* In Massachusetts, her increasingly conservative views do not go un-challenged, and "my best friend on earth is so liberal she drags her kids to every demonstration." Once a week, Beth and some of the other moms she knows who have given up their outside jobs for now get together, along with their kids. Once a month, on their regular "moms' night out," they actually get to finish a thought. They set aside one of these evenings, a few months after the '04 presidential election, to meet at Beth's place for a thorough airing of how they all voted and why.

Of the four women who arrive at Beth's door on this snowy, still night, only one has not switched back and forth between the parties during recent presidential contests. Though they place themselves at distinct points across the political spectrum, it is the two who voted for the junior senator from this state who seem to feel they have the most explaining to do. Apparently, there is no need for warm-up chitchat—and from the moment Beth's friends arrive, they are not only off and running but remarkably on topic. Mary Verra is still peeling off her coat when she finds the first thing they can all sign off on: how hard they've had to work at not letting political differences damage personal relationships during the campaign. "I had one friend that I finally had to e-mail and say, 'This is affecting our friendship and hurting my feelings,'" Mary says. "But she just wrote me off, like, 'Oh, you're a Christ-ian, so of course you think like this'"—and thus support George Bush. In fact, Mary had concluded that the country was "in a mess" and had been looking for a reason to switch back to the De-mocrats in '04, but she never found one and ended up sticking with the president.

"And did you find you could have better conversations with

women you weren't even as close to?" asks Jill Rock, who voted for Kerry. "I had one woman I was close to say, 'I don't like conflict, and I don't want to talk about this.'" Beth, who is urging tea and treats on her guests, thinks that's an excuse. "I think women just say they're not political" and back out of such conversations not because they fear conflict but "because they don't know the amount of the federal deficit. If they're not William F. Buckley or Hillary Clinton, they don't even want to say they have an opinion, because they don't want to admit it's based on a gut feeling." Which it often is.

Jill, a former retail buyer, says that though she did vote for Kerry, she could best describe herself as a fiscal conservative; her all-time political favorite was Massachusetts senator Paul Tsongas, a moderate Democrat, who died in 1997. "I was all over him," she says wistfully. She grew up in rural Oregon and outside Rockford, Illinois, in a pro-NRA household. But when she moved to Chicago as an adult, she came to think gun control sounded like a pretty good idea. And above all, she sticks with the Democratic Party over abortion rights: "I didn't choose a party," she says, distancing herself from the larger package. "I chose an issue."

The other Kerry voter, Meghan Umlauf, a dance teacher originally from Connecticut, volunteers, "I am more conservative since I became a mom. I would rip the belly-button ring right out" if her daughter—who is a toddler at this point—ever came home with one. "I am a liberal person," she says. "I vote like a Democrat, but I mother like a Republican. I run my house that way. Children thrive on consistency and structure and rules."

At this observation, everyone leans forward, as if the boat has shifted; on this, they have to hear more. "*Is* that Republican?," to be a good mom, Beth asks. Truly, if careful mothering is considered a Republican trait even by Democrats, can our political self-esteem possibly get any lower?

"Bush was the dad, and I'm sure he was shaking in his boots,"

Meghan answers, "just like I am when I punish Madison. He was pretending to be confident." But that's what good parents do, she goes on. Although in the president's case, she is not even sure he's the one really calling the shots: "How do we know Bush isn't a puppet?"

As with so many of the women I talked to in the Midwest, the way even the Bush voters here respond to that question double-damns the Democrats, because just four months after electing him, they have almost nothing positive to say: "He's not clever enough to be a puppet," says Mary, though he did get her vote. Mary taught middle school before she became a mom, and has concluded that Bush "has some kind of reading disability. He's a pretty simple man, not a sophisticated guy."

When he first became president, Beth says, "I wasn't ready. I wasn't there yet, and I was disconsolate, thinking we were going back a hundred years. But not all that much changed. And then after 9/11, I was such a fan of Rudy Giuliani's anyway, and of John McCain." At some point before she voted for him, did she come to appreciate the president himself?

Not so much. "Not everything he's done has made me proud to be an American. He's not the greatest environmental president, and I don't want drilling in the Arctic Circle." But then, "I don't think any president could make me happy on the environment, and I can do that in my own corner of the world."

Why did she and some of the others move to the right in recent years? Not one of them mentions the war in that regard. "I've just gradually gotten more conservative as I've lost my idealism," Beth says. "When you're twenty, you think we can solve world hunger." She also says the shift began a while ago, when she was a student and spent some time in England, where she felt beleaguered as an American, and was shouted at in the street on a couple of occasions. When she came back to this country it was with a new regard for our material advantages. "I appreciate that I have fifty-seven channels, though maybe there's nothing on. I'm glad I don't have only three cereals to choose from."

It does sound as though the fiscal enticements are the bottom line for her: "Democrats are for the little guy, but they want to shake down the rich and give that money to poor people? That doesn't resonate with me." At this point, the one Democrat who might be able to lure her back, Beth says, is Barack Obama. In '04, "I watched the convention, and the only person I liked was Obama, because he didn't talk about being a disenfranchised, disaffected minority; he talked about the American experience, coming here and working hard and making something."

Mary, who grew up in New Jersey, was the "hard, hard left" president of the campus Democrats back in college at West Virginia Wesleyan, but she, too, began to see things differently during a year abroad. In Vienna, she came to see herself as an American under siege in a hostile world. "Our director said, 'Do not talk on the streetcar; don't let people know you're American.' We were told if the Arabs stayed away from school, you go home," because that might be a tip-off to a terror attack.

Meghan, who also lived outside the country, working as a nanny for a Greek family in Athens, says, "I had a whole different experience; I was embarrassed" as an American. But she doesn't say more, and as the evening goes on, I notice that the two more liberal women here speak the least.

Easily the most conservative of the group, Carolyn Hildebrand, who grew up outside Philadelphia, did not register to vote until after her first child was born in '97. She describes her Republican father's politics this way: "My dad thought, 'No one else is going to do anything for me, so to hell with all of them.'" Carolyn says that on her own, she has come to essentially the same conclusion: "I almost died giving birth, but I was denied disability—and yet here are all these immigrants who got it, and that infuriated me. That influenced me. My mother-in-law drives me crazy. She's a Communist; she doesn't think anyone should be rich. Well, I'm sorry, but if I work for something, that's *mine.* Don't expect me to work for you."

Exactly, Beth says. Watching the Democratic National Convention on TV, she was so put off by all the boo-hoo speeches to that effect by "Reverend Jesse Jackson and Reverend Al Sharpton. I can't stand it! I think it's offensive to African-Americans that these guys are supposed to be the heroes. I'm sure if you asked Joe Average African-American, he'd say, 'Huh-uh.' Now, Condoleezza Rice, on the other hand—for a black woman to rise the way she has? She had to be extra crafty," Beth says, clearly meaning this as a compliment. "And she's not Hillary; she's not riding on someone's coattails."

The more of the Democratic Convention Beth watched, the more certain she became that she was no longer in the club. She felt belittled, too: "The party thinks we're a bunch of dopes. Are they saying we're the Barack Obama party or the Hillary Clinton party? With the Republicans, there's more—Everybody meshes." Mary also sees that as a positive: "There is more consistency with the Republicans."

Beth and her friends not only place a premium on meshing, but spend the evening proving that it does not require uniformity of thought. One thing that comes through consistently during several hours of conversation is their willingness to challenge one another—but always in locating points of agreement. Watching them do this is mesmerizing, and such behavior so exotic in the current political environment that it's another reminder of how sidelined women still are.

There are strong disagreements among them on Iraq, for instance. After Jill says she opposed the war from the start, Carolyn asks, "Which war? The one that started on 9/11?" No, Jill says, the one that is a costly distraction from the actual war on terror. "And I felt persecuted—for lack of a better word—that I was not really American because" she felt that way. "But isn't [Howard] Dean the one that started that?" Carolyn asks. "Before he fell apart screaming?"

Instead of walking too far in that direction, though, the women then reverse course and find something they can agree on: all they lost on 9/11. Beth and her husband visited the World Trade Center on their first date. September 11, 2001, was the first day of school for Carolyn's son, at a time when Mary was pregnant with her first child and Meghan's husband was still in the air force. One of the worst things about that day's tragedy, they all feel, is that it ended up polarizing the country. "And the sad thing is that when it does happen again, we won't pull together" even then, Mary says. "We've gotten to that point, and it's so destructive."

The issue that provokes even stronger feelings than the war is immigration. "I'm so annoyed they're forcing my child to take Spanish" in school, Carolyn complains. Jill starts to ask, "Don't we have a responsibility as a global partner—"

Carolyn cuts her off. "Why?"

"Because this country was built on immigration?"

"Well, what was true two hundred years ago isn't true now."

"When I went to France," Beth says, "I didn't call directory assistance and get someone to speak English! My grandparents and great-grandparents who came here couldn't *wait* to speak English, and what makes people crazy is people who they feel don't come here for freedom but come because 'I'm pregnant, and if my child is born here, he'll go to college for free and be on welfare forever.'"

"ESL is there because there's a need," Meghan says. "And I want Madison to learn another language."

"It's a generalization to say they don't make an effort" to learn English, Jill thinks.

Not in Carolyn's experience: "Okay, I'm at the McDonald's in Milford, Massachusetts, and I just want my chicken nuggets. And the person taking the order can't understand me. I've got nothing against him, but I want my kid's chicken nuggets!"

Everyone laughs at this, and Meghan retreats to the tried-and-true "both parties are rotten" argument. "I just don't see the difference that I can make in these elections," she says. But even the friends who disagree with her don't want to see her drop out of the system: "We need to empower you!" says Jill.

"Feel the woman energy!" says Beth.

"If you feel good about what you believe, you'll talk about it more," Carolyn needles Meghan. "It makes a difference."

When Meghan asks her friends if they think they'll soon see a woman in the White House, every one of them answers yes. Which reminds her to ask, have any of the others spent much time down south, where Condi Rice comes from? "They are some strong, strong women. They get everything they want, and they don't say a thing. I don't think it can be learned, though."

Mary's idea of a strong, strong woman is her own mom, who was widowed at age thirty-six with four kids and no college degree. Her first move was to a not-great house in a great school district. She told her children, "This will be your ticket, but you will not have everything" every other kid in the neighborhood has. Meghan feels a twinge of guilt at the memory of how hard she used to push her mom to buy her things they really couldn't afford. "I overheard her telling her sister she wished she could afford Guess jeans for me."

"So then you didn't want them anymore?" Jill supposes.

"I wish I could tell you that!" Meghan says.

It's nearly midnight, and we've been hours without even a potty break. But before we scatter, everyone wants to hear the postscript on Mary's mom, a Democrat who still mothers like—well, a really great mom. "She's the CEO of a very successful architectural firm in Philly," Mary says, hugging her hostess at the door. "She has so much money now."

The View from the Bottom

"Bush was the only one who was a
good candidate on helping the homeless."

My first surprise is that nearly all of the formerly homeless women who show up for their regular Monday-night women's group meeting on what used to be McClellan Air Force Base voted at all in the last presidential election. But I have to say, I am kind of blown away by the number who, on November 2, 2004, were living on the street and voting for the GOP. "Bush was the only one who was a good candidate on helping the homeless," says one of them, Jesse Miller, who stays now in the recycled military housing here at Serna Village, named for Joe Serna, Jr., a former Sacramento mayor who was a farm worker and running buddy of César Chávez.

Jesse is forty-three but looks a little older because she's lost some teeth along the way. She grew up in Texas and describes herself as a cowgirl, then says that had nothing to do with why she cast her ballot for her fellow Texan. "He said Democrats had too much power," she recalls, an argument that made sense to her in 2000, after—"Who was it who went with that floozy?" —Bill Clinton had served two terms. "And I didn't want to vote for Gore or Kerry." Of the latter, her impression was that "he was trying to promise to make the world a better place, but he talks so fast, I said no, I can't vote for this man; he's a liar." I could close my eyes, in other words, and be back with the moms' group outside Boston, or in the high school teachers' lounge in Fairfield, Illinois; even without a fixed address, Jesse got the rundown on what kind of candidate Kerry was.

The women of Serna Village wound up homeless in the usual ways. Domestic abuse is a highly dependable ticket to the bottom, as is self-medicating. Often their previous address was an encampment down by the American River, not far from the capital—or from the Hyatt where the governor and his wife, Arnold Schwarzenegger and Maria Shriver, stay when they're in town. While living by their wits on the streets, here where the Gold Rush began, these women lived lives more chaotic than those of us capable of stressing out in line for a latte might easily imagine. Their perspective on past election campaigns is not only the vista from the low rung of the economic ladder; it's something like the view you'd get looking up from the bottom of the ocean. And it's worth noting, I think, that for Jesse and the others here, the little bit of light that does get through at that depth all seems to be coming from the Republican Party. As a friend of mine sighed recently, "The Republicans are better at everything. Well, except governing." "Everything" in this case being another word for marketing.

Jesse doesn't remember where she picked up the impression that Bush was committed to helping the homeless, though there are certainly more people to help now: 14 percent more Americans are living in poverty than when he took office, according to the Census Bureau. But plenty of people with homes also absorbed the 2000 campaign message that Bush was a new breed of "compassionate conservative."

Four years later, the Democrats still had no catchphrase with anything like the pith and clarity of "cut and run" or "flip-flopper." A couple of months before the '04 election, my son did ask, "Mommy, why did Bush go to war without a plan to win the peace?" and for a minute there, I thought the Democrats might finally have a little alliterative mojo of their own going. They didn't, though.

Next in the circle to speak at the women's group is Pegg Knechtges, a registered member of the Green Party who voted for Ralph Nader in 2000 and 2004. "He stayed by the way he believed," she says admiringly, "and didn't drive around Washington in limousines." Because Pegg has a degenerative condition that makes it hard for her to get around on her own, she uses a walker on wheels and is trying—unsuccessfully, so far—to get on SSI. Her biggest concern as a voter, she says, is the environment, an issue on which John Kerry has one of the cleanest records in Congress. But Pegg finds him suspiciously "slick," and declares, "I wouldn't vote for Kerry on my deathbed."

Right after saying that her priorities are "clean air, Mother Nature, and not drilling for oil," she says she is nonetheless feeling quite warmly these days toward the president—the former oilman whose first reaction to Hurricane Katrina was to allow refiners to produce dirtier gasoline. Bush's record on the environment is certainly consistent: He has supported massive subsidies for oil companies in a time of record profits, broken his campaign promise to reduce greenhouse gas emissions, pushed to weaken clean air standards, and campaigned tirelessly to open the Arctic National Wildlife Refuge for first-time drilling. Still, Pegg says she can't help being taken with the way he's going after illegal immigrants. "I like George Bush finally saying something about the border," she says. "You go to the welfare office and see people of different nationalities with better shoes and driving a Mercedes." While she, a carpenter's daughter from Michigan, is turned away. Maybe the poorest among us are not so different—not in their resentments, anyway. And there is always someone worse off—rather than better off, strangely—whose imagined comforts fill us with rage.

Heads start nodding all around the room when Carrie, a thirty-seven-year-old mother of six, talks about how hard it is to live on a welfare check even if you do manage to qualify. "Kids born after '98, you can't get aid for them, so my oldest two get aid but the younger ones, no. You get five hundred and fifty-five dollars for two" children for the month. Until the five-year national limit on welfare kicks in, that is, and you are bumped off the rolls for good, as required by law since President Clinton made good on his promise to "end welfare as we know it."

These are the first women I've talked to who are keenly aware that Clinton succeeded in that. And because they know it was a Democrat who put a stop to the entitlement formerly known as Aid for Dependent Children, maybe it is not so irrational that they do not necessarily see Clinton's party as their natural protector.

Two of Carrie's sons are disabled, including one who "will be eight next month, and they just approved him" for benefits after three years of applications and appeals. "When they took me off aid" after her five years were up, Carrie started selling her blood for twenty-five dollars a pop. "I used to donate plasma, twice a week for three years, so now I've got two damaged arms. I'd drink my juice with my arm hooked up so I could have things for my kids." Carrie, too, voted for Bush. "'Be honest about your stuff,'" she says she wanted to tell Kerry. "He just didn't seem honest."

When the book *All I Really Need to Know I Learned in Kindergarten* came out, I used to say that everything I needed to know I learned from my ninety-two years of dating. And the longer I'm out here listening, the more I'm thinking there might actually have been some truth to that—and that all the premarital research wasn't bad preparation for an exploration of political life, since in politics no less than in romance, chemistry and timing regularly trump reason and a common vision.

Just like your friend who insists she is looking for a man who is a solid citizen, but can find the out-of-work landscape artist in the room blindfolded—well, it is not only homeless women who say they care most about the environment, or education, or health care, or choice, and then vote against the candidate who agrees with them. I think the clinical term is "seeing what you want to see," and every one of us suffers from it. It is not only homeless women whose choices remind us what an oxymoron "political science" is. In fact, one of the few things I can say with complete confidence to all of my fellow second-guessers who think it is so easy to run a winning campaign is: Maybe it's not.

A young Native American woman who has been stretched out across a couple of chairs on the far end of the room through most of the conversation says that she also voted in '04, but wrote in Mickey Mouse because in her view, Bush was "against Indians," while Kerry "was more talk than action." Not only that, but "he smiled crooked."

"My purpose in voting was to get on juries" to see how the criminal justice system really works, she says. "I always wanted to become a cop. But then I had in the back of my mind 'Oh, but I sell drugs . . .'" Everyone laughs; apparently, voting high and aiming for better is not exactly unheard of. As it turns out, the only declared Democrat here, other than the woman who runs the group, is Sharleyn Regino, except she never votes because "I can't see myself taking little kids" to the polling place. "But I would be a Democrat."

All of the women who live here, in one of the housing programs run by my friend Robert Tobin, are called "participants" for a reason: Like the rest of us, they are multitasking as fast as they can. They are required to perform volunteer service and get in school or otherwise on track for a job that would allow them to afford a place of their own when they graduate after two years. (Meanwhile, they pay a third of their income in rent to Serna Village, while they train for something beyond the kind of minimum-wage job at the McDonald's that would never pay enough to support a family.) They also have to stay sober and function as part of the community here, with a say in everything from hiring staff to kicking out rule breakers. Their real job is to become contributors, with all that entails.

I am not surprised when the young women I'm having dinner with mention concern for homeless people—like, yes, the Republicans at Serna Village—as one of the main reasons they are Democrats. Four of the five are Old Spaghetti Factory waitresses with the night off, tipping well at a Thai place where they don't have to bus the table. In their off-hours, four of the five are also heavy consumers of news and opinion, so they know the history of the Foreign Intelligence Surveillance Act and the fine print of the Patriot Act. Yet about a minute into the conversation, my friend Robert's twenty-year-old daughter, Frankie Tobin, who has invited the others here tonight, remarks that she had no idea how much they had in common politically because they had never before spoken about it. "With a lot of my friends, it's almost like, 'Don't ask, don't tell.'"

Frankie's coworker Christina Skillman, who is twenty-seven, says she dislikes the president every bit as much as the others do, but unlike them, she does not vote or even try to keep on top of the political news, since campaigns don't seem to be "about anything that really matters." Even the Democrats "are not trying to help with poverty or help people get off the streets or sustain life." When she listens to speeches or ads from candidates of either party, "I think they're talking about people who don't exist."

Christina's news-junkie friends focus less on specific candidates than on issues, though they do make an exception for Hillary Clinton, and are in a hurry to make clear that they are not admirers: "She's trying to move to the center, but not in a sensible way, like 'We can take care of the environment *and* help business,'" says Emily Timmons, who is twenty-six and works in Medicare billing. "Instead, she's going against flag burning." Because their focus is on policy, they don't get why so many voters imagine they'd even want to have a beer with the president—any president. "I want someone who's my designated driver after *I* had a beer," says Frankie, who on top of her restaurant job is in school at Sacramento City College.

"Well, *I* want Stephen Hawking," says Emily, but most people seem to like it when "Bush explains things that don't need to be explained." Whereas "Kerry seems like he's looking down on people, and they *don't* like that." Bob Shrum, meet Emily Timmons.

Noel Miles, who is of Polynesian descent, says she tries to disregard the candidate's personality and quirks and whole biographical narrative arc, as presented in campaign season. "I try not to look at their mannerisms, like 'Ew, why is he wearing that?' I don't want to be like that." Of course not, I think, and wonder again whether history will record that at the decisive moment, we went awry because one candidate wore earth tones and was mocked.

Noel's roommate, Mandy Barrick, who writes music when she's not handing out slabs of lasagna, feels the same way. "If the message is right, I don't care if it's delivered in a monotone. If you can do what you say, I don't care if it's funny or pretty." Not that the current president is such a spellbinder, in her view. "I tuned in to hear what he was going to say on immigration, and it was 'We need to stop immigration because we need to stop immigration, and so we're going to stop immigration.'"

"We *need* the 'No Woman Left Behind' Act," says Noel, brushing her bangs out of her face. Right, says Emily, with a side of sarcasm, because that's been a stunning success in the schools. Another concept that troubles a couple of the women around the table is this whole phenomenon of Log Cabin Republicans, gay partisans of the Grand Old Party. So Emily, who has already established her bona fides in this area—"Basically, ninety percent of my friends are homosexual; I'm a hag"—takes a shot at explaining: "Some gay Republicans have money, and they want to keep it."

True, says Mandy, who was raised Mormon and Republican but left the church and the party when she came out as a lesbian at age seventeen. "With Mormons, it's all these—no offense—stupid ideas, but you can't even have a discussion with anybody because it's all on faith and 'just because.'"

"That's why it's important to travel," observes Noel, who also grew up Mormon, in Utah. So you can have revelations like *"Oh my God, there are black people!"*

Emily can top that: "I've had people say to me, 'If you believe in gay marriage, you probably believe in bigamy, and what's next, marrying a goat?'"

"If two women can get married," Mandy wonders, "is the next step really marrying goats?"

"I don't know why," Emily says, "but it always is a goat."

They are all flummoxed, too, about why no one seems to have been able to give Bush the bad news about Iraq. Instead, Emily says, his advisers "are all like your best girlfriend, who is not going to call you up and tell you your butt looks fat." They certainly do hear the bad news from their friends who have served and come home to tell about it. Noel has one friend recently back from Iraq who "got discharged because his knee got blown up, and he said, 'That's the best thing that ever happened to me.'" Emily knows another guy who "lost his leg, which sucks because he was hot like George Clooney, and he's already been shot in Afghanistan. We're like, 'Dude, war is not your forte.'"

By the end of the night, Emily and the others are sounding almost—well, *old*, worrying about cuts in veteran benefits and lamenting that there's not more sustained coverage in the local media about the ongoing problems in New Orleans. "I'm for taxes" to pay for all the things that make government work, Frankie says, and Emily continues the thought: "Infrastructure!

Levees!" After all the tax cuts, Frankie says she's already concluded that "social security is not going to be there for us. This administration thinks two minutes ahead, when we need to be thinking twenty years ahead." She has never been involved in a political campaign before, but is planning to knock on doors for Democrats in '08. The message she gets as a young woman is "We're supposed to think our opinions don't matter as much. But even if you feel no one is hearing you, if you stay home, then they won"— once for sure, and maybe twice.

So next Election Day, "we are driving you, Chrissy," she says, patting her nonvoting friend's back. "Even if your decision isn't my decision," Noel adds reassuringly. Chrissy is not so sure: "You have to tell me who" to vote for, she says nervously. "The information isn't direct, so I can't— I have no idea what they're saying. It's all the same, so I can't decipher it at all."

Her friends all promise they're going to keep talking about this stuff and help one another process it. On the short ride back to her apartment, Frankie says, "If you never get asked about your opinions, you might never know what they are. From the time I was three years old, my dad was asking me what I thought. Even if it was that I wanted a Barbie, we were talking about ideas. But if that doesn't happen, maybe your ideas never come out."

Bad Catholics for Kerry

*"I could not swallow the Republican
stance on anything else."*

Though the Vatican finally announced just this year that
there is no such place as limbo, many Catholic women in
this country would beg to differ. Jamila Spencer, for instance, describes herself as "literally ripped in two" while waiting
for the Democrats to "diversify" and let a few more pro-life candidates into the club. Meanwhile, she looks at the two parties and
asks herself, "How can I choose between the poor and the unborn?" Jamila, who is twenty-five, works for the Colorado
Catholic Conference as a liaison to parishes, and she has already
gone back and forth between the parties several times. Recently,
she switched her registration again, this time back to the Democrats. "There is at least some history of pro-life Democrats," she
says, laughing, "and *no* history of Republicans for the Poor."

Catholics are not only the demographic I happen to know
best; they are close to being the must-have swing voters without
whom it is notoriously hard to win the White House. Which is
why George Bush has spent years learning how to pander to us
better, with excellent results. One thing he has grasped fully is
that while abortion is an important issue for many people, it cuts a

little differently with Catholics. Why is that? Because church doc-
trine holds that the protection of life is a "foundational" issue, a
kind of theological trump card. And because, unlike many conservative Protestant churches, the Catholic Church is still full of
deep-in-their-heart Democrats who end up voting Republican
over this issue alone. Under more direct pressure from inside the
church in '04 than in any previous race, Catholics ended up favor-
ing the devout, though slightly indeterminate, possibly evangelical Bush over the Catholic Kerry by 53–47 in 2004—a significant
shift from 2000, when Gore took the Catholic vote 50–47.

In Washington, I talked to one Catholic pro-life Democrat
who took a leave from her public policy job to volunteer for Gore
in 2000, as she had done for other Democratic nominees in previous presidential years. In '04, however, this woman—who thought
it would be a bad career move to let me use her name—not only
did not campaign for Kerry but could not bring herself to vote for
him, solely over the abortion issue. What had changed since
2000? To answer, she refers to a story Al Gore tells when he talks
about global warming, about how a frog thrown into a pot of boil-
ing water will jump right back out, but a frog that's been in the
water as it heats won't jump out, even as he begins to boil. (We're
the frog, get it?) Anyway, this former Gore volunteer uses the
story to illustrate how "I was the frog in the hot water, but I'm the
counterexample; at some point, I realized the temperature was
going up, and I finally did jump out."

One of the final straws, she says, was when the rumor that
Kerry was going to ask John McCain to be his running mate tore
through Washington. She was astonished that for Democrats,
"the only issue was 'As long as he promises he won't do anything
on abortion'" then that would be fine. "That was their only issue
with him." She couldn't bring herself to vote for Bush in '04, either; she's a Democrat. Nor could she support Kerry, and "my
friends who are pro-choice Democrats don't understand it; they ac-

cuse me of becoming a single-issue voter. But I say no, the party has become a single-issue party. And when Kerry says, 'I oppose abortion, but that's not how I vote,' on what other issue would we accept that? 'I'm personally opposed to racism, but . . .' No. I finally realized it had gotten too hot, and I jumped out." Those in the party who have written off voters like her could not be more wrong. But I'm going to let women caught in that bind explain exactly what it would take to get them back.

Just ahead of us on line in the Denver café where Jamila and I have met up, a woman in Lilly Pulitzer and very, very good jewelry, whose thighs are the size of my forearm—and not in a good way, in case that's not clear—is wondering, just casually, you know, if they might serve some fun little nine A.M. shots of Kahlua in the coffee, because it's so unnerving, dropping off the kids for their first day of school. All the time she's making jokes, and making things worse, the rest of us in line frown intently at the menu board—oh, cappuccino or mocha?—as if we haven't heard a thing. "Poor woman," Jamila says softly, back at our table, full of compassion for the poor in spirit, too.

"Of *course* I identify as a feminist," she volunteers—"as a pro-life feminist, though most people think that's an oxymoron." Sometimes she gets so exasperated by both sides, even on the abortion issue that's so close to her heart, that she feels like walking away from politics altogether. For instance, when she sees the NARAL folks marching around outside the state capital with signs that say, NOT EVERY SPERM IS SACRED. Or when her own supposed compatriots counter with similarly uplifting messages. "What really makes me mad are these people with pictures of fetuses," she says, grimacing. "Where's the dignity in that?"

But then, she says, she thinks about the women who fought so hard for her right to vote—and to be a part of the whole unlovely process—and she tells herself, "If I cast politics aside, that would be a slap in the face to those women." One irony for Catholic women like Jamila, who describe themselves as eager to find a way to vote Democratic in future races, is that while the wider culture tends to view them as second-class citizens in the Church, marginalized in the narrows of Catholic orthodoxy, they see themselves as marginalized by the party they'd love to call home—over the one point of Democratic orthodoxy that is no more open to debate than the ordination of women is in Rome.

Jamila is never tempted to bolt the Church; she speaks of how valued she feels there, and mentions the Virgin Mary's "unbelievable role in salvation history" with the most devout wonder. "The highest place of honor in the Church is not the priesthood; the highest place of honor is sainthood, and some of the greatest saints of the Church are women. I'd like to see our culture embrace a woman's gifts like that." To change the culture, of course, you have to vote and then work to make it count. It's to that end that in the last few months, she's convinced five friends to switch their registration to the Democratic Party. It was easy, she says, because she can explain her reasoning in two words: Bill Ritter.

Ritter is a popular former Denver district attorney who was term-limited and is running for governor as a Democrat. He is also a pro-life Catholic, though he says "that is not part of my agenda." Jamila calls his candidacy "the most exciting thing that could happen," and early polling shows him well ahead of his likely Republican competition, Congressman Bob Beauprez. But his party has told him they will open the money spigot only if he changes his mind on abortion rights, and party leaders all the way up to Hillary Clinton, Ritter told me, have tried to recruit a primary opponent for him. He is up against "this beast of influence," as Jamila calls the pro-choice lobby. During her first go-round as a Democrat, she says, "I never felt NARAL had just one seat at the table of the party; they *run* the party. I'd go to peace and justice events and have to talk about reproductive rights."

She's sorry, too, that even if Ritter is spared a primary, he can expect to be disadvantaged by a gay marriage ban on the ballot in '06—a measure expressly designed, in her view, to boost Republican turnout. "I don't agree with gay marriage, but that's no excuse to be hateful, and a ballot issue like that just invites people to sit with their hatred. Why would we exploit an already vulnerable community like that? Because we want some random guy to be governor? Marriage is threatened because my mom and dad couldn't figure out how not to cheat on each other and ended up getting divorced, not because ten percent of the population has a same-sex attraction. My deal is, who cares?" Jamila's voice is distinctive, but her lament is not.

"I'm with the Democrats on ninety percent of the issues. But if you're pro-life, they don't even want you," says Kelly Dore, whose husband Tim Dore, is a lobbyist for the Catholic archdiocese here. Because of her husband's job, "we get calls from wacky people all the time, saying, 'We wish someone would kill your children.'" And this from the party that preaches tolerance? "I've seen him giving speeches on how we need to be more accepting of different opinions" on abortion rights within the Democratic Party, "and people want to rip his head off. It's kind of ugly." Kelly says she herself "used to be more pro-choice" before she had kids and worked in social services.

People do change. Why can't the party? That's what Cindy Gurbenhoff wonders, though she seems even more put out with some of her church leaders right now. Cindy assures me I'll have no trouble picking her out in the Starbucks where we're meeting; there might be another thirtyish blue-eyed blonde in the place, but "I'll be the one who's nine months pregnant." She and her husband, who is a pediatrician, also have an eighteen-month-old daughter, and Cindy works part-time for now, fund-raising for a nonprofit. She reflexively crosses her arms over her chest as she says the word "Republican."

"I could not swallow the Republican stance on anything else," she says. "Their position on the war was a big deal for me, and I think Democrats are much more likely to protect the environment and look out for the poor instead of the wealthy. Yet on the life issues—I *definitely* don't agree with the president on the death penalty, but I am Catholic, and there was lots of stuff going on in the Church, saying you can't vote for a pro-choice candidate and call yourself a good Catholic. It really upset me that the church could just say, 'You can't vote for John Kerry,' because as far as I'm concerned, it isn't pro-life to vote for George Bush. I agonized—it's about being a new mom, partly—and thought, 'What am I doing to make the world someplace good for her to live?' So I felt I couldn't just not vote, either."

She and four of her closest Catholic women friends gnawed on the issue for months without ever coming to a completely satisfactory conclusion. "I ended up writing in Bart Stupak"—a pro-life Democratic congressman from Michigan—for president, she says, fiddling with her silver necklace, "but at least I was able to participate without going against my true beliefs."

Though she obviously takes Catholic teaching seriously, she was not at all okay with how some of her church leaders handled themselves during the '04 election season. "That was the most upsetting part of the whole election process for me. First I heard the news on TV that the bishop in Colorado Springs"—that's Bishop Michael Sheridan—"had said if you voted for a pro-choice candidate, you were sinning. That really upset me; I've got lots of friends who aren't Catholic, too, and when something like that comes out . . ." She lays her head in her hands for a second.

Cindy is one of five kids—doctors advised her mom to abort a younger sister for health reasons, though both baby and mother came through fine—and her family is as strongly Republican as her husband's family is strongly Democratic. "And they get along great, and we just try not to talk about politics. But I *love* my in-laws, and to hear a bishop say they're sinners and going to hell? You could hardly say something more ridiculous to me."

Her own bishop, Archbishop Charles J. Chaput of Denver, "never quite said that, but he didn't disagree with it, either, and he adamantly came out saying you should not vote for a pro-choice candidate, and if you're a good Catholic, you won't. I wanted to hear him also talk about George Bush and all the deaths in Iraq. Why wasn't he telling the whole Catholic population of Denver about that?" For the first time, she found herself wondering about the other-than-spiritual motives of church shepherds. "I really felt—I don't know if 'abandoned' is the right word—but they weren't even interested in the reasons why you shouldn't vote for Bush."

She doubts that Kerry and other Catholics in Congress who vote in support of abortion rights are unconflicted on the issue, but imagines that they literally cannot afford to reconsider. "When he says he can't impose his religious beliefs on the country, what I hear him saying is 'If I say I'm pro-life, I'm going to lose all kinds of money'" from the pro-choice lobby. "I think that's a huge reason why Kerry won't adopt a more middle-of-the-road stance." The real money question: Is there such a thing on this issue? Aspiring pro-life Democrats hope so, and they say that a little respect would go a long way. But in concrete terms, what does that mean?

For starters, it would require understanding that what pro-choice women genuinely see as a hard-earned freedom, pro-life women genuinely see as a self-inflicted wound—and a human rights issue comparable to slavery. If you truly believed that abortion was a cruelty to women and children, wouldn't you oppose it, too? I personally know only one pro-choice woman who uses the ugly "M" word when discussing the issue. "I suppose it is murder," she says. "But it's necessary sometimes." Sort of like torture, one supposes—which the White House absolutely does not approve of, except when it does. Real respect would also have to translate into support for a guy like Bill Ritter, the kind of pro-life Democratic candidate who is routinely run off the public stage these days.

Meanwhile, among Catholics who care what the Church teaches about sex and babies, there is some pride in the outcome of the 2004 presidential contest. A perverse pride, some would say. "Catholics prevented a lifelong Catholic from winning the White House," exults Chris Rose, another young lobbyist for the archdiocese of Denver, who ran as a pro-life Democrat for a seat in the Colorado statehouse that same year. Chris lost his race, too, though he concedes that it may not have been abortion politics per se that kept him from succeeding his first time out. "My attempts at humor did not always go over," he says, and tells about the time an older woman grabbed his arm at the Jefferson County Fair and said she had to talk to him about abortion. "And I said, 'Marilyn, I would hope that in your condition, you wouldn't need one.' But she didn't laugh, and no one else did, either. My wife, being a loyal wife, laughed."

Still, in the bigger picture, Chris sees himself as victorious. "A Catholic Democrat was defeated by Catholics," he says again, reveling in a scenario that "would have been unthinkable to Al Smith." As Chris, too, is both a Catholic and a Democrat, why does he think this is such a good thing? "Had John Kerry been elected, it would have made clear to Catholic politicians that you can work against your church and still win the highest office in the land." Instead, what it made clear is that no Catholic Democrat is likely to win at that level anytime soon—not as long as the Church goes all out to defeat dissenters on abortion, and the party does exactly the same thing.

Kerry, it must be said, did nothing to help himself with his coreligionists. On the contrary, even some supporters found his whole slapdash "I was an altar boy" lack of seriousness on the topic insulting; was Catholicism the one thing in life Kerry had *not* overthought? His Catholic problem only deepened after he told *The New York Times,* "My oath is to uphold the Constitution of the United States in my public life. My oath privately between me and God was defined in the Catholic Church by Pius XXIII and Pope Paul VI in Vatican II, which allows for freedom of conscience for Catholics with respect to these choices, and that's exactly where I am."

Kerry's mistaken reference to Pope Pius XXIII—there has been no such pontiff—might have been written off as a slip of the tongue if he had on any other occasion spoken more coherently about his faith, but that never happened. The Church unambiguously regards abortion as an "intrinsic evil" and has for millennia. One can disagree, of course, but not within the Catholic tradition. As Notre Dame's Father Richard McBrien—nobody's idea of a conservative—lays out in his *Encyclopedia of Catholicism,* "Even in the earliest years of the Christian tradition, abortion at any gestational age was regarded as a grave sin . . . the Church asserts a moral position it regards as unquestionable: even though we are not certain when the soul is infused, hence when a human being truly exists, it is gravely sinful even to risk committing murder. Hence it is seriously wrong to terminate the life of a human zygote, blastocyst, embryo, or fetus." Vatican II in no way changed that.

When I meet Denver's archbishop Chaput, who spoke out so forcefully during the campaign, in his quiet office in the chancery, the late-afternoon sun coming in through the window is hitting him square in the eyes, but—is this a corny cosmic joke or what?—he doesn't look away. And when he looks back on the '04 election, it is with equanimity, maybe, more than anything. "One thing I do hope flows from this," he ventures, "is that we all come to understand that labeling ourselves Catholic doesn't mean we are. It isn't a heritage we receive from our families; it's a choice we make personally. . . . I've never been convinced that the fact that someone says 'I'm a Catholic' or 'Gosh, I was an altar boy' qualifies them to claim that they are Catholic. And we're all sinners, of course. But it's a different kind of violation of God's law to claim that the law doesn't make a difference than to break the law."

But is it enough to say "Gosh, I'm pro-life"? I'm curious about how he feels about Bush's statement as a candidate in 2000 that the country wasn't ready to overturn *Roe* v. *Wade.* Or about the fact that both Laura Bush and Barbara Bush have clearly identified themselves as pro-choice. I personally have long since concluded that George W. Bush has no interest in seeing *Roe* thrown out because that would mobilize the pro-choice opposition and alienate the prosperity wing of his own party, the big-business crowd that is his truest constituency. How confident is the archbishop that Bush and his party are really on his side?

Chaput's answer is precise but indirect. "Twenty years ago," he begins, "the argument that, you know, abortion is just one of the issues probably could have been more acceptable to Catholics who thought that there would be steady work on the life issue along with other social justice issues. But pretty soon, that became an excuse to do nothing about the life issues. And so the refusal to vote for a pro-choice person means something different today than it meant twenty years ago."

That the issue is not even on the table for some Catholic candidates seems to bother the archbishop most. "If those same parties would be willing to *discuss* that issue, even though they have a position, along with other social justice issues—you know, how do we improve the criminal justice system, how do we take care of the poor, how do we handle the abortion question—then there would be more credibility. So I think in some ways, the more aggressive stand of some of us during this past election period . . . was the result of seeing that any other kind of stance hasn't gotten anywhere."

The Catholic lobbyist Chris Rose was right, I think, when he said, "Republicans have done a great job of creating the moral consensus on abortion, but ending abortion isn't something they know how to do, because that would require an enormous change in our country and in our government," including programs to help women provide for their children and avoid unwanted pregnancies. "And if you believe government can't do anything right, then you *can't* end abortion."

So, again, is the archbishop so sure of either Bush or his party? He sighs. "I've never spoken about either candidate personally, but I would say that theoretically, someone who says they're against abortion is further along the road to doing something about it than someone who's indifferent to the question. . . . You can have good Catholics who say that they're not for the criminalization of abortion, or they want to take gradual steps towards eliminating it by convincing the public that this is a bad thing. Those are all legitimate political positions—as long as you're really moving towards the goal of protecting unborn human life. You at least have to have the goal."

Chaput, who turned sixty this year, insists that all the national attention to his statements about abortion during the campaign took him by surprise. "On one level, it was uncomfortable to be called a Republican when I'm not"—and astonishing to receive a more heated and prodigious response than even the clerical sex abuse scandals provoked. "Do I think there are people in the last election who voted for a pro-choice candidate and did so sincerely after serious reflection and prayer? Yes, I do. Did they do wrong? No, they followed their conscience. But that serious reflection and prayer, that's really important, and not just being swayed by party sympathies or that's the way you always vote. It has to be about the issues." If he could go back to '04, is there anything he would do differently? "I regret that people were hurt and offended," he says, "but I wouldn't change anything, and I have a clear conscience."

As far as I can tell, so do Democratic leaders, who continue to go out of their way to give needless offense. As when Democratic National Committee chairman Howard Dean dragged Catholics into the whole argument over intelligent design, despite the fact that Church teaching is in no way incompatible with what science teaches about evolution. On the CBS Sunday show *Face the Nation,* Dean took this shot: "Science is science. There's no factual evidence for intelligent design. There's an enormous amount of factual evidence for evolution. Those are the facts. If you don't like the facts, you can fight against them. The Catholic Church fought against Galileo for a great many, many centuries." To review, he is reaching back four hundred years for exactly the right insult? Excuse me for wondering if anyone who invokes Galileo even wants our support. Though the poor guy's case was plenty complicated, his name has become universal shorthand for "Catholics are charter members of the Flat Earth Society." And if the Democratic Party cannot do better than that, they will likely go on losing presidential elections—with their purity intact.

The "Strident Pro-Choice Money Women"

"He is a fabulous candidate in all other respects."

By seven-thirty A.M., Beth Strickland's airy, art-lined living room is filled with gorgeous women of all ages, in chic business suits and tennis wear, picking at almond croissants and fresh fruit. They are smiling, yes, but the speaker, Democratic gubernatorial hopeful Bill Ritter, knows what he is in for, and even before the intros are over, the former Denver D.A. is sweating through his blue dress shirt. "I don't know that I've ever had an introduction that sounded so much like a rebuttal," he jokes, and the "strident pro-choice money women," as he's described them to me earlier, all laugh. (I know, I know, respect *is* supposed to cut both ways.)

As it turns out, it is one of the few light moments of the morning, to no one's surprise. These Democratic activists can make or break a candidate—by opening their wallets or not—and the issue on the table alongside the pastries this morning is among the most serious facing their party: Just what do they do with a guy like Ritter—so capable and charming and, let's cut to the chase, *electable*—but so off the ranch when it comes to abortion rights?

In the past, the pat answer has been to run from such a candidate, even if the result is the election of a conservative Republican. But since John Kerry's '04 loss—and the "values voter" discussion it sparked—Democrats have been rethinking how well that approach has worked for them. Among party centrists, there is at least a grudging admiration for the way the other guys have managed to have it both ways on the issue, whipping up their Christian base without ever having to deliver in a way that would activate the opposition.

But here, at the other end of the spectrum from the evangelical crowd, these equally true-believing women do not think it possible that Bush has been bluffing. They have not only been using the specter of back alleys and bloody coat hangers to raise money for thirty years; they are genuinely fearful that *Roe* could be reversed, and with deadly results. Like their political adversaries, they see any compromise as potentially calamitous. And for some of these voters, too, the issue is nonnegotiable.

Yet in the reduced circumstances in which the Democratic Party currently finds itself, others have concluded they might have to try something new. So, with many misgivings, they have come to hear Ritter out, maybe slap him around a little. And he is thrilled to get the chance to let them; it is a first step.

"To get anybody to come, I had to say in the invitation that it's *not* an endorsement and *not* a fund-raiser, because we're all strongly pro-choice," Ritter's friend and fellow lawyer Ann Frick tells me in the kitchen before the event starts. "And since then, of course, Sandra has retired"—Justice O'Connor, she means—"and Rehnquist has died, so the situation has changed," and not to Ritter's advantage, obviously. Ann's cohostess, Marla Williams, who is also a friend of Bill's, is at the sink cutting the last of the fruit. "If we lose *Roe* v. *Wade* at the federal level, it's even *more* important" to have a pro-choice governor. At this, Ann groans, she is so conflicted. "He really promoted women in the D.A.'s office," where she used to work with him, "and those are *notorious* boys' clubs. He is a fabulous candidate in all other respects, bright and articulate and a man of the people."

And big and handsome in a rugged, Mountain West kind of way, with quite a bio: His dad was a heavy-drinking heavy-equipment operator who had a small wheat farm on the side, out east of Aurora, where Ritter grew up the sixth of twelve kids. After his father left them, Bill went to work at age fourteen, doing construction to help support the family, and he put himself through college and law school that way. Near the end of his father's life, he not only reconciled with him but took him in. And when Bill's own firstborn was a baby, he and his wife spent three years as Catholic volunteers in Zambia, teaching women in villages about nutrition. He also passed out condoms in Africa, to help stop the spread of AIDS, which means that he is insufficiently pro-life for his Church.

Out in the foyer, Leanna Clark, a PR exec who served with Ritter on the Denver Public Schools Commission on Secondary School Reform, didn't catch what Ann just said but echoes her almost exactly: "I have so much respect for him; he's brilliant, and I think he'd be a fabulous governor. But even for me, it's challenging. And for some of my friends, it's a brick wall." Which shows in the body language of the guests here, many of whom prefer to remain standing for the program, leaning against the living room wall with their arms crossed over their chests.

"Plenty of room to sit here on the floor," Beth calls, but almost no one moves; no one wants to be in the posture of sitting at the candidate's feet. She kicks off the intros with what can only be considered a qualified recommendation: "He's very electable." When it's Ann Frick's turn to speak for Ritter, she cannot fail to mention that "there are some things I clearly disagree with Bill about." Third up, Marla Williams is the toughest of all: "We disagree on some issues that are core to my value system. . . . It puts me into a very difficult quandary." Ritter responds by giving her a hug.

Leaning against the piano and looking like he'll take any support he can get, he starts by reassuring the crowd that they have no differences on gay rights, a matter Marla mentioned as one area of concern. "Good!" the room replies. And he supports using embryos that would otherwise be discarded by fertility clinics for stem cell research. Another group "whew." But then it's on to Topic A: "First of all, in the world of media, they use an expression for me that has either been 'pro-life' or 'anti-choice,' but there's more to it than that. And the people who've said there's no difference between me and Bill Owens," Colorado's current Republican governor. "That's absurd." Ritter wants to restore the Planned Parenthood funding that Owens cut, he says.

He goes on to tell about how he hired many women lawyers in the D.A.'s office. He started a job-sharing program there, too, and major prevention and police training efforts on sexual and domestic violence. He's all for providing access to emergency contraception, and speaks at some length about how underinsured women are, how critical it is to fund education and child care, and even women's athletics, given that "we know elevating the educational level has a big impact on preventing unintended pregnancies. We know women who participate in sports have fewer unintended pregnancies."

Speaking with his hands wide apart, at chest level, and bending at the knees every few beats, he looks as if he's playing an invisible accordion. "As governor, you put out a vision, and I think my vision would make a difference to women." The closer to the heart of the abortion debate he gets, the faster he's pumping up and down. "So let's get to the real issue: How is it you're considered by the papers to be anti-abortion? And it's a fair label. I would veto an absolute ban, but I would consider signing a ban with exclusions for rape, incest, and the health of the mother. That's the place where I've come as a matter of conscience." One woman asks why he can't let his conscience dictate his own "private actions" and leave others to do the same. Otherwise, his position "doesn't work for me, I'm sorry," she says, and her voice cracks. "Sorry," she repeats. "I didn't know I'd be so emotional." A second woman says that Ritter's inner struggles notwithstanding, it "seems like it *is* a political decision."

Oh, no, he tells her. "The easiest thing politically for me to do is to be somewhere else on this" as a Democrat, and there is a murmur of assent on that. But then a woman who identifies herself as a pro-choice Republican says, "I'm not clear on what you're saying. Maybe I'm the only one who missed something."

"No, you're not!" a bunch of other women shout out. "Would you sign a ban" on legal abortion or not?

"With exceptions, yes," he says.

"Well, then," the lone Republican answers, "I don't understand how you reconcile saying it's not political with saying you would sign that bill." What he means, he says, is that it's not a politically advantageous decision for him. "It is a matter of conscience, and I struggle with it. That's why I say it's not political. Does that make sense?" No, a woman across the room answers, "*none* of what you're saying makes a damn bit of difference if a child or young woman becomes pregnant. We live in a culture where thirteen-year-olds watch *Sex and the City* and *Friends*, and then we provide no options? We're giving such mixed messages." She shakes her head. "To me," reproductive freedom "is the gateway to everything else that happens." It is a foundational issue, in other words—a theological trump card.

The only other man in the room—who is willing to sit on the floor, and so is looking up at Ritter—says the former D.A. simply hasn't walked his argument far enough down the road. What about fatal or even nonfatal fetal abnormalities detected by an amnio? "To stop with the life of the mother is a big cop-out," says the man, who identifies himself as a doctor and asks if Ritter is planning to put doctors who do abortions in jail. No, Ritter says meekly. "I don't think anyone should go to jail, and I understand your point. But I have a brother who is severely retarded and— It's something I'll think about."

"So, what's your answer?" several women call out at once.

"It's not something I'm going to decide here this morning," Ritter responds.

The murmuring in the room is growing louder and unhappier now with each question. What do the words "emergency contraception should be available" really mean to him? Does he think birth control should be covered by Medicaid? And what about those pharmacists who refuse to fill scripts for the morning-after pill? When he answers that last one by saying the state has no real power over pharmacists, the collective room temperature goes up again. "I'm just not sure you can, legally—that's the thing about thinking like a lawyer," Ritter adds, taking another shot at it. That's why "I testified *against* the parental notification bill. I took a stand, but it was a lawyer's stand."

One woman who has not spoken before says, "Look, you have many positive attributes, and compared to what we have now, you look like a God—" Before she can finish the sentence, the Republican cuts her off: "Not to some of us," she cracks, and the room erupts in laughter.

But that's only for a second, before they notice that a woman leaning against the far wall has begun to weep. Then everything goes very, very still. "It is *deeply* humiliating," the woman says quietly, "that you don't think *our* position is a position of conscience. We *all* have a conscience about this."

"I apologize. I didn't mean to humiliate anyone," Ritter says, and in a back corner of the room, another fellow prosecutor, Lynn Brilliant, stands to defend him. "I am sure there are women in this room who have had to wrestle with this on a personal basis, but he'd *never* take that away." She is quickly shouted down, though: "He said he'd sign the bill!"

A dark-haired woman in a black suit, who keeps her arms folded as she speaks, says furiously, "I'm desperate to get here with you, but I'm fifty-nine years old, and I know what it was like before *Roe* v. *Wade.*" When he answers, Ritter looks not at her but at the woman who is crying. "I can't tell you how much I understand what you're saying. I'm just trying to be really honest, and if I lose an election over this, I lose."

A woman who says she has worked for years with Planned Parenthood indicates that she would not mind that outcome at all. And since prohibitions don't work, she wants to hear his plan for dealing with all the abandoned children and "women who hurt themselves" if abortion ever is outlawed.

"There are nuances," he says.

"Not that many," says the Republican.

"Actually, there are," says the woman from Planned Parenthood. "They're called people."

At what seems like a critical moment, Ritter's friend Ann tosses him a lifeline: Would he support Democrats who *are* pro-choice if he were governor?

"I believe that Democrats are the people who care most about life" for the already born—"that's *why* I am a Democrat," he thunders. Then, allowing himself a wan smile, he goes on, "And I don't know that I've ever supported a pro-life candidate, because I don't know any other pro-life Democrats."

This has gone on for over two hours, and some people are leaving, off to work or workouts. Even Beth, who lives here, slips out for another meeting, urging everyone to stay and talk all day if they want to, and by all means take some brioches home with them. Before the group completely breaks up, a couple of women who were still undecided when they came in offer endorsements. "My mother is a good Catholic lady who's been voting Republican, and she would vote for you," says one of them.

"I am enthusiastically behind Bill," says another—"and

choice is my number one issue—because of the integrity he'll bring to the office. Bill Ritter is the guy who defeated parental notification in this state. When our health centers were vandalized, he's the D.A. who aggressively went after the perpetrators. Women stand to gain so very much with you as governor. I feel like the most pro-choice thing I can do is vote for you—then work to keep abortion legal and keep that legislation away from your desk, or break your hands before it gets there, if necessary."

Elaine Berman, a former school board member whose first job was at Planned Parenthood, stands and says she's decided to support him, too. "I'm a pragmatist. I want someone who can win, and Bill Ritter can win. I wish he felt differently about choice, but there are very few politicians who are principled like Bill is." The woman who mentioned her work for Planned Parenthood earlier does not see it that way. "I'm *not* ready to make that compromise," she says, looking right at Ritter.

Marla says she has to hand it to her old buddy. "There are very few candidates who would get up in this room." But she seems no closer to deciding she can support him. "Bill, I know you care about poor people and young people, and those are the people who will bear the burden" of a ban on legal abortion. The woman in the black suit seems angrier than ever. "You wouldn't jail them," she says of abortion doctors, but "you'd just take away their livelihood?"

The woman who has enjoyed this morning most thoroughly is the Republican in the room, and she exits laughing. "Your candidate is very entertaining to me."[14]

14. According to the November 8, 2006 *Denver Post,* "Democrat Bill Ritter trounced Republican U.S. Rep. Bob Beauprez on Tuesday in the race to become the 41st Colorado governor—completing a stunning year-long transformation from the party's unwanted candidate to its leading figure." He did so with the support of many of the strongly pro-choice women who were in the room for this tense first meeting.

Not All Wedge Issues
Were Created Equal

"Oh, no, here comes Father and we haven't
even talked about abortion."

The Catholic sisters who make up the tiny Anawim Religious Community of the Bethany Retreat Center have chosen to live slightly apart, on a wooded acreage here, with a Marian grotto and a prayer labyrinth. They are not cloistered, however, by any means; they run a school, direct spiritual retreats, treat the sick at a clinic and homeless shelter, and follow the national debate, almost always unhappily. The current Senate contest here between two pro-life candidates is an unexpected pleasure, and one they'd like to linger over, like an impossibly rich dessert. But they do not even hope for such a thing in '08, and fear far worse: Sister Suzanne Thibault, a lifelong Republican so mild she shouts, "Oh, *sugar*!" when annoyed, posits that if Hillary Clinton were nominated, "She'd get killed, literally assassinated. We have too many right-wing people out there who would do that."

Some people would consider Suzanne herself right-wing, and certainly, she and the others here do hold up the conservative end of the Catholic conversation. Yet of the half-dozen strongly pro-life sisters and laywomen talking around a table one morning on the retreat center's cool and dimly lit lower level, two went with

153

Kerry in '04, and two more indicate that they might still vote for the Democratic nominee in '08—if, they say, the party chose someone like John Edwards. That this is the case among such traditional Catholics is a measure of just how gettable more middle-of-the-road believers are.

As for Edwards, I had nearly forgotten that guy, but they haven't. "He was my favorite; I thought he was honest," says Lillie Rees, the center's wry longtime receptionist, who was so unmoved by her choices last time that she stayed home from the polls in '04. Nicole Fedder, a ponytailed young Republican who works in the office here, seconds that: Edwards "had that family appeal." For their quieter coworker, Carol Anne Socash, "he had the charisma Kerry didn't have. I voted for Kerry because I thought Edwards would give him what he lacked." Edwards also supports abortion rights, so what happened to abortion as insurmountable? He seems to have spoken to several of these women on a level that made them want to look away from the issue they call their top priority, just as Bush was able to do with those women who said they cared most about health care or the environment, then voted for him.

Nicole's husband, who works at a Wal-Mart distribution center, had to cut back on their insurance coverage recently. He had almost let it lapse altogether right before Nicole, who is thirty-one, had what she refers to as "a form of a stroke. They thought it might be from birth control"—nobody flinches at the reference—"but I said it was stress." She still doesn't know for sure and isn't likely to find out anytime soon. Because her insurance no longer covers it, "I'm not going to my specialist, and I can't get my MRI this year." At least until now, no issue other than abortion made it onto Nicole's screen. "I find out who is pro-life, and all I know" beyond that "is Gore was the whiner and Bush is the Texan, the better-looking guy. I can't even remember who he ran against last time. See, I don't know anything."

"And yet," Lillie remarks dryly, "she's been talking for twenty minutes." What Nicole does know, once she's reminded that his name is John Kerry, is that she so distrusts him that she wonders whether the fellow soldier whose life he saved in Vietnam was paid to appear alongside him at campaign rallies. "People think soap operas are real. They don't know he might have paid that person to be there and hug him." Whereas Edwards, she says sympathetically, "only lost because he didn't have the money" to get past Kerry. Here, at least, Edwards seems to have done what every Democratic candidate tries to do, which is get voters like Nicole to make something other than the abortion issue the measure of his character.

Sister Ruth Ann Madera was already with the Democrats in '04, not because she's changed her mind on life issues but because she no longer believes that the president is nearly as pro-life as advertised. "The first time, I voted for Bush because there was an e-mail going around about his Christian values, and I believed it!" she says, as if she's spent a lot of time since then mentally copying, *"Ruth Ann was wrong."*

"The second election, no way I could vote for the man, because he *uses* being pro-life. Texas is first in capital punishment, and that bothers me, and the war bothers me. It doesn't add up. That e-mail," she says, shaking her head, "I was so impressed." Democrats typically argue the opposite, that Bush is a committed—indeed, obsessed—pro-lifer who would stop at nothing to see *Roe* overturned, so they aren't likely to see the sense in Ruth Ann's argument. But that view of Bush, sold everywhere by Democrats, has been quite an effective advertisement for the Republican Party.

The other two sisters at the table would not likely vote with the Democrats under any circumstances, though they are not exactly Republicans, either. Sister Karen Willenbring, who is a medical doctor, runs a free clinic where "I see diabetics who have gone without insulin for one or two years," she says, and tells about a carpenter she treats who has been buying his pills a few at a time. "I'm certainly not a happy Bush fan," she adds, pulling her white sweater closer around her. "I contemplated not even voting, but then that whole thing kicked in." Guilt, she means. And abortion is far from Karen's only problem with the Democrats: "I'm very much against experimenting on embryos; they're people. That could be you, you're frozen, and they're doing experiments on you." Nicole sighs, and says, "The life of a tree is more important than the life of a person." But Ruth Ann, who has been listening to this exchange with one finger to her lips, argues, "We're connected, every person and every tree." And as I always say, no planet—no place to fight about abortion.

Yet Karen's is the minority view even in heavily Catholic Pennsylvania. I have come to this swing state hoping to hear what happens to the daily discussion when abortion is effectively taken off the table, as it has been for the moment here. With a pro-life Democrat, Bob Casey, Jr., taking on the pro-life Republican incumbent, Senator Rick Santorum, that debate has gotten a rare night off. What's immediately apparent as a result is that other wedge issues, like embryonic stem cell research and gay marriage, do not begin to fill the void. JoAnn Zartman, who is the longtime president of the hospital auxiliary in nearby DuBois, says that in the last election she defected from the Republican Party and voted against Bush, expressly "because of stem cell, even though I'm Catholic and I don't believe in abortion on demand." JoAnn has spent a lot of time at the hospital over the years, and with gay couples, "it's so sad when one partner dies and a niece you haven't seen in a hundred years comes in at the end and takes over" because the surviving partner has no legal rights.

For Democrats, this Senate race is not the toughest matchup one could imagine.[15] Though a hero to conservatives, Santorum was recently named the Senate's least popular member, with the

15. Casey easily defeated Santorum, 59 percent to 41 percent. Incumbent Governor Ed Rendell also beat Republican challenger Lynn Swann by a double-digit margin.

lowest approval rating and a flair for the unfortunate quote, often on the topic of gay sex. But the instructive thing about this moment in Pennsylvania politics is that we can for once see rather than imagine that when abortion is a moot point, the debate shifts not to stem cell and gay marriage but to two other moral issues: the war in Iraq and the war on the middle class.

Another evening that week, at St. Francis Parish in Clearfield, a few miles away, five childhood friends who went through Catholic school here together are meeting up. Jean, Joan, Jackie, Pam, and Susan haven't seen much of one another since their graduation in 1965. But recently, Jean—Sister Jean Ryan—who is back in town caring for her mother in their home across the parking lot from the church, realized that the others were all back, too, and started talking about a reunion for which I provide the excuse. Some people, it's true, might hesitate to jump into a big political discussion after forty years, but when you've seen one another through all of the sacraments shy of the one most of us still think of as the last rites, a certain comfort level is probably permanent. So, my priest friend who lives at St. Francis vacates the living room, decorated in the timeless Early Rectory style that argues against my notion that the priesthood is teeming with gay guys. As the last of the five friends from the Class of '65 arrives, Pam Hertlein jokes that she had better get her say in now, before Jackie Gilliland takes the floor. "My father was a union member," Pam says, "so I'm a Democrat to the core." Which takes Jackie by surprise: "I never knew that about you."

Well, Joan Domico says, that's "just like I saw Pam's picture in the paper and said, 'What's a nice Catholic girl like you doing in the Lutheran choir?'" Not that there's anything wrong with that, she hastens to add. "I don't really believe *everyone* should be Catholic," even if "I know we're the only ones going to heaven." (Yes, she is kidding, though as I write that, I can also hear my southern-born friend Rose telling that "behind every little tease is a little bit of truth.") "I'm a Democrat, too," Joan says, "but I have Republican leanings."

Jackie translates: Joan might have a little thing for the former Pittsburgh Steeler Lynn Swann, who is running for governor as a Republican this year. "She went off to a dinner for him, and I saw her an hour and a half before, and she didn't tell me!" Jackie is sort of a Democrat, too, she says, "but actually, I'm not for either party. I'm thinking of starting my own." Which would make Joan's life easier; she owns a beauty shop in town and finds that political tensions even there have become so acute that she has started trying to schedule her customers so the strong Republicans and the strong Democrats don't have to run into each other. At the shop, Joan reports, "You still hear people say 'Bush has a plan'" that we just don't know about for success in Iraq. "There are still normal people like us who think that?" asks Susan Buck, who also moved back to town to care for her mom. Susan is a registered Republican but has pretty much had it, she says, over the war and "a lot of other things."

At the moment, Iraq is only the second-hottest topic in Clearfield, a town of six thousand on the Susquehanna River in the middle of the state, between two ridges of the Allegheny Mountains. And it's not any of the prescribed "life" issues that these former St. Francis girls want to talk about. They don't tarry on memory lane, either, though I love hearing about the turkey tarts they had to make in home economics class, and how Sister Mary Evelyn let them know that Jackie Kennedy was a woman not to be admired. Instead, they cut quickly to the matter uppermost on their minds, which is not the Mexicans moving here but the jobs moving there.

Jean starts to say something sympathetic about the plight of Mexican immigrants—"If my family were starving"—but doesn't get to finish the sentence. Pam, who spent "thirty-five years, seven months, and two days" of her life turning out men's suit coats and blazers for the Bayer Clothing Group, cuts in, "Excuse me! My job went to Mexico, so how can they be starving?" The same thing happened to Susan, whose job at Berg Electronics in Emigsville was packed up and relocated to Juarez; she works as a cashier at the Sheetz gas station here now. Of course, their story is the story of blue-collar America—Pennsylvania lost 20 percent of its manufacturing jobs between '01 and '04, according to state labor statistics—so it's no wonder globalization is front and center. Joan tells how she heard that some of the Americans who were sent down to Juarez to train the Mexicans who were replacing them—gee, why would there be any hard feelings?—came back and reported that their trainees "hid in the bathroom." Which shows, Pam says, that "they don't really want to work."

Jackie, who for many years lived in Maryland, where her husband was a state trooper, did nonprofit work with migrant farmworkers in apple and peach orchards there. "And the other side of that coin is I've never seen an Anglo pick a crop. The truth is, I never saw one white person picking—and for minimum wage, and with the way they live, on cots?"

When Pam lost her job, she says, she did get some retraining. "But when you start over, you start over at half" the salary. "And I went to school for medical assistant," only there were no jobs. So, she says, "When I watch *CSI* now, I can say, 'Oh, I know that!'" Jackie says Pam should still be proud of herself "for taking advantage of the schooling; I'd probably just have chucked it and gone for the housewife thing." But Pam has a hard time feeling that anything came of her efforts: "So here I am, old, and I hold nothing against them"—her former employers—"because they did what they had to do." Where she works now, at a Head Start program where she does the accounts receivable and makes 60 percent of her former salary, she's starting to get the feeling that layoffs might be coming for her a second time. "I can just feel it in the pit of my stomach, that here we go again."

On the subject of money and security, Jackie remarks that it must be nice for Jean, who has worked in Guatemala and Haiti, and with the Navajo out west, to have "been all over the world, but in the convent, you don't have to worry about the bills." Jean says nothing, and Jackie continues, "I don't know how you guys felt about high school—I was the hellion," she explains to me— "but those of us who lived on the East End of town," who were Italian, mostly, along with a few African-American families, "we always felt like outsiders, especially in the Catholic schools."

"I never knew that," Jean says quietly. Jackie never forgot it: "Sister Evelyn said, 'I never liked Italians.' When I told her I heard on the radio that the president had been shot, she made me sit in the office for telling a lie. What it comes back to is, the town was divided." Given the current circumstances, it's not so surprising that unseen foreigners thousands of miles away loom so large here now. But Jackie's memories are a reminder that there is always an outsider closer to home, too, even in a town that is 98 percent white, even in an immigrant church.

My priest friend comes back in then to see how we are doing, and Jackie says, "Oh, no, here comes Father and we haven't even talked about abortion!" Nor do they, other than to agree with Joan that "it will never be solved politically." They, too, seem to support embryonic stem cell research, nodding agreement when Jackie says, "If your daughter were hurt, you'd be for it." And they don't mention gay marriage, but end the evening by roughing up the one-man, one-woman kind a little—you know, just teasing: "Or, how about this, even if he watches what you have on, he has to hold the remote?" Jackie says. "Oh, and he's got to sit *here*." Pam wonders if maybe "that's what happened to Bush with 'Stay the course,' and he can't change now.'" Because he has to hold the remote and sit *here*.

Then again, constancy is often seen as its own reward. "Our girls, in our whole class of nineteen, are all still married to their first husbands," Jackie says proudly, though it was she who had argued earlier that the Church ought to be more accepting of those who are divorced, like her daughter, and Joan's. "These guys," she says, looking around the room, "are probably what you'd call real friends, and that's what brought me back."

The next day, by coincidence, I meet another member of the Class of '65, Mary Hurd, who went to the public school in town. "The Italians and the blacks lived together on the East End," known back then as Spaghettiville, says Mary, who manages the Kwik Fill and is still one of only a handful of African-Americans here—"fifty in a fifty-mile radius. East End was always considered the bad kids and the rough kids. Jackie and I were good friends." When I ask her how much things have changed since then, she laughs. "Most whites in this area think there was never a race issue, but they don't see the little things, the people who won't take change from you or, if they rub up against you, they jump back. When fair week comes, it's like they never saw me before."

Mary talks politics every day with her little morning coffee club at the Kwik Fill—the warden from the jail, two guys from the highway department, a couple of day workers, and one guy on disability—"and we get into it pretty good." Her biggest issue, she says, is definitely economic. Congress has to increase the minimum wage: "I'm an employer, and right now I have someone who is going to have to quit because she can't afford the gas" to come and work at the gas station. "Most of my workers work two or three jobs, trying to make it with all the factories gone, and I have one who is a nurse and cleans houses who never has a day off."

But I should be used to it by now: She is a Republican, out of respect to her father, she says, and gratitude for the opportunity the party gave him a long time ago. After World War II, "my father came home from the military and was high up in the army but couldn't get a job" commensurate with his skills because of his skin color, so he worked as a janitor and a driver. "But he was a

Republican, and that's how he finally got his job" with the state Department of Transportation. He later became the first black teller in the local bank.

"Mary, would you get out here?" one of her regular customers calls from the counter, and she leaves her office in the back of the store to wait on him. When she returns, she allows that despite her strong party loyalty, "I resent the government right now because they make me feel stupid" for having voted them in. So even she is gettable for the Democrats—for the right candidate, that is. "I was against the war because I didn't think we had enough proof" that Saddam posed a real threat, "and I actually had decided on Kerry. But the more I listened, I just couldn't believe some of the things he'd say, and I thought he didn't believe them, either." There it is again: Kerry didn't seem to believe his own line, and there is no overcoming that.

Before I leave town, I want to see Jean Ryan again, and we visit in her kitchen, where you can look out the window and see St. Francis church. Jean says it was Susie, the quietest of the five friends from the Class of '65, who had stayed in touch with them all over the years. "She comes down here every night" to hang out with Jean and her mom, who is ninety-seven. Jean had been away since she left home at eighteen to join the Sisters of the Blessed Sacrament, and it has been "kind of hard" coming back after so many years. "Just down the river, we have one of the worst coal-burning plants, and the mercury from that," she says, giving a shudder, "but we can't question it because you heard them last night, talking about jobs. When I first came back, I said, 'Let's check the river,' and everyone jumped on me and said, 'Why would you want to do that?'"

The thing is, it's impossible for her to ignore what she sees as an overarching moral issue. "I look at the universe as the body of Christ," and feels an obligation to care for creation. Politically, "even the Democrats anger me, and it isn't only that they won't express the issues, it's that even when we're talking about the economy, it's *our* economy," and too bad for the other guy, she says, her elbows on the table and her hands clasped behind her head. Yet she does feel at least somewhat hopeful, she says, "because since the Big Bang, we've never been static, and out of death comes new life. We almost need a major catastrophe to move us out of our lull."

I do occasionally argue during these noninterviews, but only if I really agree, and I ask Jean if this isn't just the liberal iteration of my high school friend Kim's laissez-faire belief that even if we are poisoning the planet, "maybe that's how this planet is supposed to end."

"Oh, no," Jean says; we have a responsibility to be anything but passive. Yet "spirituality is finding meaning in chaos," instead of struggling to stay impossibly in control. "I don't think a lot of people are touched by chaos," she says, which results in all sorts of sexual craziness, for example. It's not an example out of the blue, though. Because while Jean is here nursing her mother, she is also recovering herself, from the trauma of having to report a sexually predatory priest in the Philadelphia diocese, where she was bullied and belittled by his defenders before she was finally proven horribly right.

The daily routine—sacramental, really—of caring for her mother has slowly restored her peace of mind, Jean says. "She's a great woman, she's buried two husbands, but she can laugh at herself and still pushes herself, and it's good to watch somebody age like that, with grace. I was angry when I came home, and this has helped me let go." She imagines that she herself is barely recognizable from the girl she was when she left Clearfield so many years ago. "When I first entered the convent, I didn't want to change the habit," to drop the traditional dress, which at that time included a half-veil. "You had three—a Sunday, a daily, and one for the doctor. And now I'm considered liberal in my own community. Jackie said last night I've been around the world and never had to pay my way, but I've worked and never been paid, either. You'd work for a year for maybe two hundred dollars." And when Jackie expressed pride that none of the women in their class had been divorced, "I thought, 'But I wonder at what cost?'"

She sees the convent as "a true communistic society," as well as a dying one. "We're dinosaurs; we've had maybe one a year taking vows." Yet she tries to look for signs of life after death there, too. "In the beginning, religious life challenged the Church. Now it is an arm of the Church, and you need numbers to be that." So, she concludes, "the B-and-B's"—Pope Benedict XVI and the Bushes—"are bringing us to a new reality." Both spiritually and politically, they are unwittingly clearing the decks for—she doesn't know what. Yet she has faith enough to believe in whatever comes, very much like my friend Kim, though from quite a different angle of entry.

Before the women from the Class of '65 went their separate ways the night before, "Jackie said we need to talk about this religious stuff," to figure out what they do and do not truly believe at this point in their lives. Jean suggested that they start meeting regularly as a group, reading *In Search of Belief* by Joan Chittister, a book that goes through the Apostles' Creed phrase by phrase and offers some alternative interpretations of the traditional prayer.

For these childhood friends at age sixty, looking with baby eyes at questions Sister Mary Evelyn taught them to disregard at sixteen sounds like a potentially upsetting thing, and maybe even the tender shoot of new life that Jean is looking for. "I could see last night we're coming from different directions," she says, "but that's okay."

Kitty Dukakis Revisited

"Michael always says I'm too hard on John."

I f life isn't fair, political life is particularly unsporting. So in lieu of a second act, Kitty Dukakis takes in the show, missing nothing. In the interest of learning from history, I pay her a visit and find the wife of the former governor and '88 Democratic presidential nominee Michael Dukakis trim and toned at age sixty-eight, appearing at her front door in black jogging shorts and a purple tank top. Just back from a run through the neighborhood where she and her husband have lived for forty-two years, she apologizes for the shorts and the sweat: "I just kept running into people." Their granddaughter, who is staying with them for the summer, is still asleep upstairs, so we keep our voices down in the kitchen, where Kitty—who insists right away that I call her that—warms up some coffee in the microwave.

"Do you listen to progressive talk radio?" she begins. "Michael says I'm addicted." A timer goes off just then. "Oh, that's Michael's bread. He's going to be seventy-two in November and still teaches year-round. It's a subject I go cuckoo about." Now, it is slightly startling to hear a woman who has made headlines as an alcoholic, who relapsed on rubbing alcohol during her husband's campaign, and who wants to destigmatize electroshock therapy treatments for depression, refer to herself as "addicted" and "cuckoo" before even taking a seat beside me at the kitchen table. But though she's much less careful than anyone who is still in the game, she does not seem at odds with herself. In fact, as she goes on, I begin to think of her as a kind of blue-state Barbara Bush without the spleen, a truth-talking wise woman of the party who recognizes the necessity for change even as she embodies some of the same Old Democrat thinking that she herself says Democrats need to let go of.

The Republicans, by her lights, have won over a lot of women by default, while her guys barely put up a fight on the issue she considers paramount, health care: "The Democrats don't make the case! We don't do real grassroots campaigning in every precinct in the country so that when it comes to health care, folks will have the information" that it's the other side's clubby relations with insurance and pharmaceutical companies that make medical care unaffordable and inaccessible. After her husband left public life, Kitty went back to school to get a master's in social work and became personally involved with trying to help immigrants get access to better care. She doesn't understand, she says, why her side so cavalierly writes off whole swaths of women who so obviously could be won over. "We have to accept the fact that there are people who are going to be agin' us on abortion who need us on health care, who whether they're evangelical or not, are not getting health care."

Like most Americans, she worries about the troops in Iraq, in particular one of her husband's favorite students, whom she does not fully believe when he e-mails to say he is fine, fine. Though she would not have put Saddam at the top of the list of ongoing threats, there are a few spots in the world where she feels we should be more involved, not less. "The situation in Darfur," for example, "is unconscionable, and *women* are the ones who should be united on this, to make the words 'never again' mean something." She has served on the board of the U.S. Holocaust Memorial Museum and spends a lot of time as an ad hoc advocate for refugees, traveling to the Thai-Cambodian border to bring back orphans. While we are talking, an immigrant she describes as a "doctor from the Middle East, working here as a waiter," calls to see how she's coming on helping him with his papers. "Women need to be louder" on humanitarian issues; those in public life are barely heard on the subject, and she thinks that's because in politics, as in all of life, women still try too hard to please. "We've got to push ourselves much more" to be unpleasant when necessary and then "to be able to take the criticism" that inevitably follows.

When I mention the criticism leveled at Teresa Heinz during her husband's presidential campaign, Kitty smiles and says, "I went through a little bit of that." She rates her own handling of bad press during her husband's presidential race as decidedly "mixed." "I learned early on that if I was going to be honest, I was going to be criticized, but Paul [Costello, her press secretary] taught me, 'The press doesn't want garbage from you. They want what you're really thinking.'" (Note to Paul: Where are you when we need you?)

Overall, Kitty says of her time on the campaign trail, "It was a real growth experience." Ouch, in other words. She saw clearly enough that her husband "was in trouble as we got on in the campaign, and I went through short periods of time in the campaign when I was depressed. The drinking stuff had begun, and though I didn't realize it, I was beginning to get into real trouble. It wasn't pleasant, and I have good reason to be angry; when I went into treatment, someone dropped a dime five minutes after I got there. But I hope John Kerry's wife looks beyond this" kind of criticism of women on the public stage, she says, circling back to the point of departure. "We have to be able to take the barbs and develop a thicker skin. Women have to get angrier." Are we insufficiently angry? There's no lack of outrage for men or women, is there, on either side of the aisle? But we are not angry in the right way, she argues—not in an informed, targeted way.

And what's with calling Teresa "John Kerry's wife"? Doesn't she know her any better than that, living right here in Boston? Kitty rubs the back of her neck before answering that one. "Teresa is not a woman's woman, not warm and fuzzy, or I've never found her so. But she has other qualities, and it's not easy being married to John, I'm sure." When I burst out laughing, she walks that back, but only a couple of centimeters: "Michael always says I'm too hard on John." Husbands, right? But hers, she says, has only grown on her. "He's been incredibly support-ive of me with some issues that have been hard." It's with his help, she says, that she has fought depression and has been sober for four years now.

So it's more than a little ironic that the moment that crystal-lized his failure as a presidential candidate came when he answered debate moderator Bernard Shaw's question about how far he'd go to defend her: "Governor, if Kitty Dukakis were raped and mur-dered, would you favor the death penalty for the killer?"

"No, I don't, Bernard," Dukakis responded, branding not only himself but his fellow Democrats as stereotypical liberal fraidy cats. "And I think you know that I've opposed the death penalty during all of my life. And I don't see any evidence that it's a deterrent, and I think there are better and more effective ways to deal with violent crime. We've done so in my own state." His low-affect answer had quite an effect.

For Kitty, that defining moment hasn't faded much over time. "That was sixteen years ago, but it's like it was yesterday. I re-member what I had on and how, when he looked over and saw my expression," he knew he had just driven off a cliff. "I was furious. We were in the car with our daughter Andrea afterwards, and I said, 'What were you thinking?,' and he said he was so tired and had answered the question so many times on the death penalty, and it was just automatic. Andrea went on and on about it, and I remember thinking he was going to be burdened by that from then on, even by his supporters. You're so exhausted, and you're going to make mistakes."

Yet though he flubbed his one chance to rhetorically tear a theoretical attacker limb from limb, he has in real life protected his wife all these years. "His understanding about women," she almost whispers, "is something the public didn't understand."

Which is maybe why some of the trivial things that used to aggravate her about him no longer do. "This weekend, we went to a bat mitzvah, and he was coming there from a Greek event for Olympia" Dukakis, the actress, who is his cousin. "So here he is in a tux, coming from the Green Line. He took the streetcar from the Four Seasons because he was not going to take a cab! Forty years ago, I would have been furious." And now? "He takes plastic bags with him and picks up paper on his way to work." She shrugs, as if this sums up everything. "And now I'm doing some of that, too."

Kitty is also trying to learn a few new tricks from her three grown kids. One big thing she's working on is better understanding people of different political persuasions. Her daughter Andrea, an NPR reporter in Colorado who is married to a Republican, "is helping me with that. Andrea is asking me to respect—not to accept but to respect—that there's another part of society."

The classic northeasterner in the liberal bubble that is Brookline, Kitty suggests, probably does come across as insulated. "Andrea tells me, 'You don't even know anybody who doesn't think the way you do.' But on day care, on you name it, we have to come together with people who don't think the way you and I do on choice and gay marriage," she tells me. Her assumption that someone in my line of work must agree with her on choice and gay marriage suggests she's right to realize that her daughter is on to something.

But this is not just talk; she and her husband will be campaigning for the pro-life Bob Casey, Jr., in Pennsylvania, she says. "I adored [Casey's] father, and both of us said we had to accept he had a different opinion" on abortion rights.

What America has responded to in Bush in the past, she feels, is not so much his conservatism as his whole brush-clearing, down-home thing, which she describes as "his inarticulateness and his ability to put his arms around people and joke and be a cowboy. And I'm not being critical of cowboys," she adds. For a minute, I think she's making a joke, but then I think not. "But they might not have women's best interests at heart," she goes on. "Our candidate in '08 needs to have a *real* open ear to issues that are meaningful to us." Amen on that.

On the subject of Hillary Clinton, she takes a deep breath and seems unsure what to say. "She was not one of my close friends as a gubernatorial spouse," she ventures finally, "but I have great respect for her." The current first lady, in any case, is even less a favorite. "I hope women will *not* take a page from Laura Bush," she says, and makes a face. "I don't see anything evil about her, but we're very different women." That's despite the fact that, as she notes, "Lynne [Cheney] and Laura and I are all Thetas."

She does feel for Laura Bush when she thinks about what the pressure in the White House must be like. "I heard from someone who knows that she started smoking again during the campaign. So, she's human, too." The acknowledgment, however grudging, that we are all flawed and conflicted and in this together is at the heart of the Democratic Party—and the thing that scares some people away.

In the Navy

*"Nobody, I think, would put several hundred
thousand people in a conflict for oil. Even if
it were Clinton, I wouldn't think that."*

Before dinner, Elizabeth De Angelo and her friends take a
minute to sit back and contemplate the bowl of Italian
meatballs her husband, Nick, has prepared—in complete
faithfulness to his father's recipe, though he has tweaked his
uncle's sauce with a little ground pork and made it his own. The
De Angelos met in ROTC and married the month they graduated
from college five years ago. They shipped out soon after the wedding but are on shore duty now, and live near the base here in
what feels like a honeymoon cottage, in which every room has a
theme: One is medieval, complete with a suit of arms, and another
is dedicated to their alma mater, Notre Dame, with a mural of the
Golden Dome on one wall.

The three other young servicewomen Elizabeth has roped into
coming over to talk politics tonight all have babies, and as she is
eager to start a family, too, the conversation naturally gravitates to
breast-feeding—"Is a thimble of wine okay or no?"—and postpar-
tum weight loss. Though I've come here to hear about their expe-
riences in the war, it's jarring all the same when the talk finally
does tack from day care to the Persian Gulf. "I was on a guided

missile destroyer, and we were shooters; we had Tomahawks," says Angela Vasquez, a twenty-seven-year-old officer from Selma, Alabama. "We were over there the first night and launched the first missiles, and it was really exciting. I hated to think— You're far away, so you kind of distance yourself from what's going on on land. But you try to focus on the end result and hope it's a better Iraq."

So, the "shock and awe" missiles that made my babies cry were fired by this nice mommy? Bad, bad Melinda, I know, sexist in the extreme. But these young women are not free of conflict about their roles as nurturers and sailors, either; on the contrary, as they describe it, that's part of the deal. I'm here hoping to learn how they—the real security moms—feel about our mission in Iraq and the government that sent them into it. Has their experience in the military reconfigured their politics in any way, or can even IEDs accomplish that?

Growing up on a marine base, Camp Lejeune in North Carolina, "I had a very strong conservative father, so that influenced me. That's what I thought I was, and still today I identify more with the Republicans," Elizabeth says. Her views have grown somewhat less conservative in recent years, and she says that's mostly as a result of her marriage. More often, wedding vows seem to have the opposite effect; married women are getting more Republican all the time. But Elizabeth says that although her husband is more conservative than she is, the give-and-take of their relationship has helped her sort out where she stands, closer to the political center. "He's a sounding board, and he's not my dad, so I can really talk to him" and change her own mind in the process. Sometimes she changes her husband's mind, too, as when she convinced him that supporting the death penalty was inconsistent with opposing abortion rights. "So I've actually become a little more Democratic-leaning."

The war has had no discernible effect on her politics, she says, because she does not see it as a partisan matter. "Being in the military opens your eyes that it is dangerous out there, and you have to believe that no president would want to run the government into the ground, for their legacy, if nothing else. So if a Democrat did get elected, I wouldn't think, 'Oh, *no!*' I don't know if the reasons we went over there were the right reasons. But even though I didn't like Clinton as a person, I can't believe— Nobody, I think, would put several hundred thousand people in a conflict for *oil.* Even if it were Clinton, I wouldn't think that. I think they do what they think is right."

The faith she has in a commander in chief she didn't like or trust, in any other context, is greater than the faith some of us have in the leaders we choose to support. Though the evening has just begun, this is, I think, the bottom line for an awful lot of political noncombatants who weren't altogether sure we should have gone into Iraq, but *are* convinced there must have been a rationale that seemed solid at the time.

Much of the rest of the world does not have this kind of confidence in the rationality and best intentions of its leaders. But Americans do; in fact, we insist on it. Just underneath our thin protective coating of "they're all corrupt" cynicism is a deep, deliberate—stubborn, even—and paradoxical belief that our better angels will somehow carry the day, no matter which chowderhead is elected.

When we ask ourselves, "Is this a man of faith?," that's a stand-in for a much more basic question: "Is this a fundamentally good person?" On that one point, we must be satisfied, too, in no small part because we are then so willing to serve up a super-sized portion of benefit of the doubt. (One of the reasons we judge sexual lapses so much more harshly than other failings, I think, is that it's pretty hard to put a good-faith spin on that.)

And when it came to Iraq, we had much more than the president's word to go on; to believe that we went into this particular war for anything other than upright reasons would be even more incomprehensible because so many Democrats seemed fine with it at first. "At the time, so many senators were for it" on both sides of the aisle that it doesn't seem right to hold only one party accountable now, Elizabeth says, untying and retying her long hair in a loose bun. "That just bothers me."

Though virtually all Democrats, and many Republicans, too, have united against the war at this point, "They were wrong first!" isn't much of a rallying cry. It's still unclear how much any Democrat who voted to authorize military force might benefit in '08 from Republican mistakes in Elizabeth's war, which she witnessed from the deck of the U.S.S. *Kearsarge*. "We were carrying marines over," two thousand of them, for the initial invasion of Iraq, and were anchored off the coast of Kuwait.

The night the war in Iraq began, Elizabeth stood on deck watching Angela's Tomahawks. "I'd just gotten off the midnight watch, and I thought, 'Oh, this is crazy'"—wild, she means, and awe-inspiring. "We walked outside and saw the missiles flying, and I'm thinking, 'It's neat; this is history,' but at the same time, I'm also thinking, '*Holy crap.*' You really hope what's happening is for a good cause, and you really *have* to have faith in our politicians. . . . It's definitely a psychological thing. You don't go to war by yourself, and you'd like to believe your war is a just war, or you think you're a criminal. To do your job, you have to believe."

At that same moment, "I was an ensign driving a billion-dollar warship," says Angela, who is so committed to the mission that the navy should put her in a commercial. (And she is way more impressive than those guys in the army ads, with all their talk about how sending your kid off to war will help him "be the man.") "We shot missiles and defended my country and told other ships to move, and I felt almighty and all-powerful, and I loved it," Angela says. "If you stop thinking of your family for a minute, it's an awesome job. You are out at sea doing things other people dream of. I have really mixed feelings about going back," but that's only because she has a ten-month-old daughter. "I work in an office here, and they all go, 'You're going to get out now that you've had your baby,' and I *hate* that."

Mitzi Mattox, a slight woman who probably still gets carded at twenty-five, grew up in West Virginia and enlisted right out of high school, but she can't wait to be discharged in two years. "Some people it's meant for; I'm ready to try something new." Elizabeth smooths her napkin a couple of times. "I have to be honest, since I'm not a big fan of the navy overall, and say that the whole pregnancy and family thing is why I'm getting out" this summer, when her five-year commitment is up. The men in the navy see a woman pregnant in the uniform, and they look at you like 'Slut.'" Keri Mitchell, too, put in her resignation recently, right after she came back from maternity leave, though her superiors pressured her to stay in and go back to the Gulf. "Now everyone is going over; it's ridiculous we are spread so thin."

When I ask if military service has changed their political views in any way, Angela answers first. "I've always been a Republican," and serving in the military, "you're more apt to believe there's a good reason" to go to war. But Keri says though she went into the navy "a firm Bush supporter," she exits a critic. "You can't play all sides," as she feels this administration has done. "Funding was cut so much on my second tour, people were bringing toilet paper from home! Yet at the same time, he's cutting taxes, and the deficit is ridiculous."

Mitzi says that though she's never much followed politics in the past, "now I feel offended by the way Bush handles things. We did our job and went in, but there has to be a limit. Who is going to protect our home front?" And Keri says about the only thing she's sure about at this point is that the public does not yet have all the facts: "Everything is kind of fuzzy." When explaining the rationale for the war, Bush "used to have a point," in her view.

"But now it's just mushy"—and it's the military men and women and their families who are suffering most as a result. "My dad is air force, and all the wives my mom knows have husbands who are gone all the time; they forget they're even *human*. And my dad says there *is* a draft," in effect. "I signed on to serve my country, but I didn't sign away my soul."

Even Angela thinks an exit plan ought to be in the works by now. "That area of the world has been fighting since before the Bible was written." In fact, when she gives her larger read on the situation on the ground, I could almost close my eyes and think this was a critic of the war talking: "I'm from a small town, Selma, Alabama, and we've got a black mayor now, and he loves to say, 'Whitey is keeping us down,' because if he keeps everybody angry at white people, he gets to keep his job. And it's the same thing in the Middle East; somebody is making money." The war "has got to be benefiting *somebody*—the top Al Qaeda guys or somebody—otherwise, why?" There are plenty of brutal regimes in other corners of the world, she notes, "but they don't have oil."

All that said, she stops short of questioning the motives of current American leaders, and instead blames the out-of-power Democrats for the fact that, as she says, "the military has fallen down in the planning" of this war. "Clinton did a lot to harm our military." The public figure she and the others here seem highest on happens to have been one of Bush's closest advisers at the time we invaded, Condoleezza Rice, who was intimately involved in planning the war. "She is crazy smart," Elizabeth says, "and I love that she's secretary of state, but with fashion sense: 'I am walking around with my boots on.'"

The military makes Angela feel a little like that—proud of herself—with boots or without. "My mother was in the navy, too—she and my father were both enlisted—and I remember watching her every morning, putting on her girdle and her skirt, and I was mesmerized. I was in awe." Not long ago, she says, she and her mom were together in southern California, "and the little gate guard didn't salute me on a base in San Diego, and my mother leaned over and gave this guy an ass-chewing like I'd never seen before. She said, 'You deserve that salute, because you wear the uniform.'"

Actually, all of these women feel they are due a small salute, in a way that one sees all too infrequently. But Elizabeth speaks with even greater pride of what her sister, Julia Reintjes, who is also in the navy, has done during her tour in Iraq. "Julia is a combat nurse, and they'd fly out the wounded. She'd fly in the helicopter, and she had to learn how to do it all with no lights, to listen for people's breath and feel their injuries." Back in their ROTC days, Elizabeth remembers, "we made fun and called the nurses fake military. The last time nurses deployed was Vietnam," so Julia naturally thought she'd get a hospital posting, in Germany, perhaps. As it turned out, "she and the other girls trained with the marines, and she had to carry a nine-millimeter."

At the evening's end, Elizabeth invites me to come back in a couple of weeks, when she and Julia and a couple of other nurses just back from Iraq will be meeting in Norfolk for a spa day. So on that day, after they've treated themselves to the world's hardest-earned manicure, facial, and massage, we meet for lunch in a café. "Is anybody else greasy?" Elizabeth asks, running a finger over her freshly exfoliated skin. "Moisturized," Julia's friend Stephanie Higgins says. Stephanie, Julia, and another friend, Christina Carmody, served together in Iraq, but none of the three is big on war stories. "Everybody asks me what it was like," Julia says. "I say, 'There were good days and bad days, and I'm glad to be home.' There's no way you can describe it in a way that people want to listen to."

"When you're taking care of a patient, your focus is on that," Stephanie offers, and Julia mentions that because the waterlines at their base got bombed periodically, they had to learn to shower with three bottles of water. All of them had trouble sleeping off and on. "We're not outside the wire" at the base, Stephanie says, "but you do have IEDs going off all the time." When I ask about tending dying soldiers, Julia suggests only that it's nothing like in the movies: "At that point, they're usually not really with it anymore." While she and Stephanie were treating the wounded in helicopters, Christina was back on base, caring for their psychic wounds as a navy psychologist. She, too, plays down her role—"It was busy"—dividing her time between those who needed to see her "because they were getting blown up on convoys and were having acute stress reactions" and those who came in because "their spouse was cheating and spending all their money." The latter "was probably the majority," Julia says dryly.

Christina, a Democrat from Bethesda, Maryland, just outside Washington, says that while the war did not change her views on the issues, it did alter her outlook on electoral politics. "I traditionally am very passive as far as politics go, because I think it's all B.S. But now I see it affects your life, and now I think I need to be more active and knowledgeable. My frustration when I was over there was looking at the guys going out on convoys and wondering, 'Were they really as protected as they could have been?'" Did others in her unit feel that way? "I don't normally talk about politics with anyone."

Like her sister, Julia is a Republican. "We were raised conservative, and that's where I am, but that doesn't mean I necessarily agree with the whole war thing." Her political bottom line is not war anyway, she says, but abortion, which she strongly opposes.

Stephanie, who is a Democrat, says she, too, has mixed feelings about the war she served in: "The Iraqis we met were glad we were there, but they were behind the wire," on the American base, she says. "It's hard to say if we're progressing. I personally get discouraged." Though she is as strongly pro-choice as her friend Julia is pro-life, she, too, cites abortion as the issue she votes on.

In some ways, Julia says, the reality of the war has come home to her with more of a gut punch since she got back to Camp Lejeune. "My neighbors said, 'Oh, yeah, that guy died, and that guy died, and that guy died,' and it makes you sad when you see the signs welcoming you home and you know they're not welcoming everybody." She worries about her boyfriend, a tank officer still serving in Iraq, who "drives through the desert looking for weapons caches. If he sees people, he tries to scare them and points a fifty-caliber at them, so he probably does not get a good reception in terms of winning hearts and minds." But, she adds, "I don't trust anybody over there anyway, not one single person—Iraqi person, I mean; I obviously trusted you guys. But even the kids I don't trust.'"

But if she does not consider the Iraqis our allies, doesn't that mean she questions the mission? She answers a little tersely: "That's why we're training Iraqi people to provide their own security." Yet again, at some moments you could close your eyes and think Julia was an opponent of the war—for instance, when she says, "It seems like Afghanistan was just our in" into the war in Iraq. "You never hear about that."

Even for these servicewomen, abortion can loom larger than other concerns, including the war in which they've risked their lives. Their time in Iraq was life-changing, yet it was not necessarily party-changing. There was so much movement under the surface, yet none in the voting booth. And though the war has cost their commander in chief the respect of some of these navy women, it is still not clear that his party will suffer as a result in '08, particularly if Republicans nominate someone who has been critical of the president.

Over a shared dessert, I tell Christina—hey, she is a shrink—about a dream I had the night before, in which I'm back in college and taking a class from Bill Clinton, who for some reason is vein-popping mad at me, and bellowing in my direction in front of all of my classmates. He's so furious I can't understand what he's saying at first, but then I realize that it's Hamlet's "Get thee to a nunnery" speech to Ophelia. Not that I personally have a conflicted relationship with the Democratic Party or anything—no way, right? But it is a pretty straightforward mise-en-scène of the party's whole self-destructive renunciation of all the women it could so easily be holding close.

Christina has a far more interesting recent dream to tell, though, set back in Iraq. "I was holding my weapon, and I kept yelling, 'It's on fire!' It was loaded, so I kept yelling, 'It's going to explode!' But nobody did anything; I don't think they could hear me. So finally, I just dropped it. I let it go. There was nothing else I could do."

Divided We Beg

"Oh, the righteousness of menopause."

T he parking lot at the United Steelworkers of America Local 5724 is full up for a lunchtime meeting. No surprise there; workers at the two Ormet aluminum plants up the road in Hannibal have been on strike for fourteen months and counting, so not a lot of people have somewhere else they need to be in the middle of the day. Last month, the company sold off the equipment from one of the factories and announced that 600 of the 1,220 strikers had lost their jobs for good. That pushed the unemployment rate here in Monroe County up to 10.6 percent, the highest anywhere in the state. Things aren't much different across the bridge on the West Virginia side of the Ohio River, where chemical workers at PPG Industries have been walking the picket line since September. UNITED WE BARGAIN, DIVIDED WE BEG, says a bumper sticker on a rusted-out pickup outside the union hall. Inside, there's more evidence of the second part of that slogan.

Labor has been hit hard by globalization, but also by its own membership's growing affinity for the Republican Party. The first woman I approach in the union hall is Martha Leasure, who is seventy-five and tells how her husband spent his whole working life at Ormet. In a very real sense, her husband's former coworkers have been out all this time to protect families like hers; Ormet filed for Chapter 11 bankruptcy protection in January 2004, and the strike was called just before Thanksgiving that year over a reorganization plan that would have cut the health benefits for workers who had already retired.

Martha worked, too, at a mom-and-pop grocery store, Leo's, over on the West Virginia side. Leo's ran bills for years for folks who were struggling, and the owners didn't let any of the high school kids who hung out there at lunchtime go back to class hungry. But the place went under over a decade ago. "It couldn't keep up with the bigger stores," Martha says, and that was even before the local Wal-Mart opened. "It was so sad." So, small wonder that what Martha wants in a president is "someone in there for the people and not for these big corporations." When I assume that means she voted for Kerry last time, though, she corrects me. "No. I liked Kerry better, but I voted for Bush." And why was that? "Oh, I got talked into it by my son, and I've told him it was a big mistake. My son belongs to the NRA, and they had him all riled up" that Kerry wanted to take away his gun. Did she see it that way, too? "Bush was supposed to be a good Christian man, and he didn't believe in the abortion and he didn't believe in the gay marriage, so maybe I wasn't that hard to talk into it," she says. "But I guarantee I'd never vote for Bush again, even if he could run." Does that mean she plans to vote Democratic in '08? "Oh, no," she answers, as if I've said something funny. "I don't make a difference between Republican and Democrat. I just go for the best man."

John Puskar, a union troubleshooter working in the back office today, complains that more and more union members vote Republican now, though new laws pushed through by the Republican-controlled Congress have steadily weakened worker rights and safety standards and strengthened the hand of the lawmakers' corporate sponsors. "They're crying poverty," he says of Ormet's owners, "but then they give these executives bonuses after they went belly-up. And it's all Republican laws" that let them get away with it. But there is no getting around the fact that the workers are complicit in their own undoing. "The Republicans vote and get involved and make sure laws are written in their favor, and the Democrats don't do that," he says. "The problem lies in our population."

The folks milling around in the hall, drinking coffee before the meeting, did get one piece of good news when a Monroe County judge ruled that the workers were in essence forced to walk out, making the whole action a lockout rather than a true strike—a distinction that has finally made Ormet workers eligible for unemployment benefits. But the big topic of conversation here today is Robert Greenwald's new anti Wal-Mart movie, *The High Cost of Low Price,* which some of them have just seen the night before at a screening at the senior center over in New Martinsville, where the Wal-Mart is.

The senior center borrowed a big-screen TV for the night, and a local activist, Janie Poe, brought the movie, which she's been showing anywhere she can muster an audience. "Pay attention," Janie told the fifty-some people gathered there as they passed around boxes of pepperoni pizza. "Because this is a movie about what's happening in America today. We are living this movie. This movie will tell you how we're supporting slavery in China and what it's doing to us here." They minded her, too—and as they watched the documentary, murmured and shook their heads over the failure of America's largest employer to provide adequate benefits or pay a living wage. (Don't take Greenwald's word for it. Wal-Mart's CEO, H. Lee Scott, Jr., who made $17 million in salary and stock options last year, answered an underling who wondered why Wal-Mart couldn't provide retiree health benefits this way: "If you feel that way," he said in an e-mail published in

The New York Times, "then you as a manager should look for a company where you can do those kinds of things.")

After the screening, Carol McMannis, who's working on a campaign to organize retired union members in support of national health care legislation and pension protection, asked the crowd whether Wal-Mart had killed any small businesses around here, and they called out, "Sure did." "Yesterday," Carol confessed, "I needed an ink cartridge, and we live in no-man's-land, so what did I do? I went to Wal-Mart. So we've got Wal-Mart here, but we can stop having more things like this happen to us. I could not live on what they pay and raise my children, and the guy at the top makes billions. The mom-and-pop operations paid their employees, and they were part of your family and helped out" by extending credit in tough times. "Does Wal-Mart? I don't think so."

After the screening, one woman in the crowd, Barb Price, said that her first reaction to the movie was "I shouldn't go back there." But then Betty Blatt called out, "My second impression is 'Then where *do* we go?'" When I asked if anyone in the room had decided to stop shopping at the local Wal-Mart after seeing the movie, not one hand went up. After Janie reiterated the movie's point—that the way Wal-Mart keeps prices so low is by selling goods made in China, often by children working in unspeakable conditions—Betty countered, "A lot of people can't afford sixty dollars for a pair of pants."

Carol asked, "When are we going to take our country back?" but no one had an answer. "Elections are a long way away," Betty said, and anyway "How do you know your vote will be counted?" Around here, too, it seems a given that Bush stole the 2000 election and fixed the one in '04 as well. And if some people have been radicalized as a result, others have given up. "It was crooked; it wasn't legal, and I don't think the first one was legal, either," said the woman seated next to me at the screening, Margaret Hoffman.

Janie, who brought the movie, took a pass on the pizza they

were passing around; that was virtually all she ate when she was a new refugee from a rough marriage, working three jobs to support three kids. Days, she worked as a medical technician at the hospital, then stopped off to give in-home care to a young transplant patient on her way home to change for what she calls her babysitting job, "babysitting drunks" at a local bar. "My oldest son in college was working at Domino's then, and they'd give him one extra-large pizza a week, and he'd bring it to me, and that's what I would eat all week."

After the showing, we stop for dinner at the Candlelight Lounge, just down the road from the senior center, where we run into a coal-miner friend of Janie's who is complaining that there's so much float dust in the mine where he works that he's afraid they'll have an explosion like the one that killed twelve miners in the nonunion Sago Mine the week before.

"*Report it,* damm it," Janie tells him. He already has, many times, he says, and in fact is leaving management a note about it every single day, to no avail. File an official complaint, she prods, but he does not see what that will accomplish—and it's not hard to figure why: A congressional report put out by Democrats on the committee that oversees mine safety found that at the Sago Mine, there were 208 violations of federal safety rules in the year before the accident, for which the company had paid an average of $156 per citation. Since Bush took office, the Mine Safety and Health Administration had levied maximum fines just 37 times, versus 118 times in the previous five years under President Clinton. Still, her friend's "what's the use?" attitude drives the crusader in Janie, who is turning fifty this week, around the bend. She was born thirty miles away and lives up the road in New Martinsville. But she is also a citizen soldier in the liberal blogosphere, where she spends many hours a day and has become e-pals with Cindy Sheehan.

"This is a real hard area for me" because it's so conservative,

Janie says, twisting her thick honey-blond hair around one hand. "So I thank God for my computer. But my son hung up on me yesterday; he labeled me as being negative. He says, 'I go to the Wal-Mart and you give me a lecture,' and it's true. Oh, the righteousness of menopause; I'm becoming my grandmother! That's something we all have to fight within ourselves, being one-sided and thinking we know more than we do." Sometimes she thinks she needs to quit the Internet cold turkey. "It's consuming my life."

But she isn't sure how else to work for change in her corner of the world, where we drive to the Ormet plant the next morning. There are only three strikers pulling their regular shift on the picket line. They're standing around a fire in a trash can, though it's a mild day, and waving at all the cars and trucks that honk on their way by, in at least a second's solidarity. Across the road, off company property, a small handmade sign had been stuck in the ground: SCABS HAVE NO GOD. As Janie and I walk up to the strikers, a man gets out of a white van parked by the plant entrance and begins videotaping us. Another such "goon," Janie says, followed her all the way home after she stopped by here a few days ago.

One of the strikers, Joan Skees, a soft-spoken fifty-six-year-old with ginger-colored hair and granny glasses who has worked as a lab analyst here since 1978, says the workers would have done almost anything to avoid walking out. "The raise we were asking for was already going to be less than the increase in what we pay for insurance. Since '83, we've given concessions with every contract until we've got the lowest benefits of any of their plants now, and we haven't had sick days or personal days in ten years."

Still, she says, the company's decision to go back on its commitment to retirees was a stopper. And now that they've been out so long, "we don't know where we stand," other than on the picket line. "Are we even going to get our pensions? We don't know anything." Joan's husband, a roll grinder for Ormet, is training to drive a semi truck, she says, giving a half-wave to a passing car without even looking up, "and we try to find odd jobs."

Why does she think unions have become so impotent? "We've talked about that," on the picket line, she says, moving away as the wind shifts and sends ash from the fire in her direction. "Are the unions *trying* to be sold down the river? But it's just corporate greed more than anything else, and that they know they can do it cheaper overseas. I'm surprised the whole country hasn't gone bankrupt."

All in good time, says Bob Ellis, a former coworker standing next to her. Just then a car passes us on its way out of the factory's parking lot. The driver used to be the plant's union chairman but is a supervisor for the company now. We all turn to look at him, but he's talking on his cell phone, and if he sees us, gives no sign. Yet the strikers do not seem entirely unsympathetic. "Ormet hasn't treated the company people any better that they have us," Joan says quietly.

At the senior center the evening before, several people said laughingly that you could no longer find anyone around here who would admit to having voted for Bush, but that isn't true even among the families of this handful of strikers. "I couldn't believe the people even in that plant who voted Republican because of that abortion issue and that gun issue," says the third striker, Danny Snyder. "I didn't work at all in 2005, but I have a wife with a decent job." A wife who now votes Republican. As does Bob's wife, Julie Ellis, who also worked for Ormet. "Her dad helped start this union here, but she's given up" on it, as well as on her old party. Also on any hope that she'll ever get her job at the plant back. "She's just taken another job in insurance sales," he says, "but she's having a hard time."

When I call Julie later, she says that realizing her job at Ormet was never coming back was quite an emotional blow. "I worked there for seventeen years and spent more time with those people than with my own family. When I found out they were closing the place, I cried for two weeks, not even so much for the financial part as for the connection." Bob's new job as a deck hand on a river barge "is hard for a man in his forties," she says. "Men in their twenties usually do those jobs. And Bob and I have been lucky to find jobs, when so many people haven't."

It was when Clinton pushed NAFTA through that was the last straw for her as a Democrat, Julie says. Like the homeless women who noticed when Clinton shredded the safety net, blue-collar workers noticed when he, to their way of thinking, sold out the American worker. Of course, Republicans are far more closely allied to big business, and support similar trade agreements, including Central America Free Trade Agreement. "Yes, they do," Julie says. "Nobody's on our side anymore." She never expected any better of the Republicans on that front, though, so she was more disappointed in the Democrats. And when Clinton signed NAFTA, she says, she felt that all she had left were the culture issues, where the differences between the parties seem so appealingly clear, and even uncontested. "I'm an old-fashioned conservative Democrat, and guys like Kerry are off in their own little world, pushing gay rights to the max."

Julie Ellis is plenty representative of the American worker's loss of faith in the Democrats, but the member of the Ellis family whose job best sums up the future of the American worker might be Bob and Julie's grown son in China, who teaches executives how to speak English. "And these are the CEOs of an *American* company," Bob says, like he would laugh if he could manage it.

Then Janie and I head to the union meeting up in Clarington, where she is mobbed by people who want to know when they can see the Wal-Mart movie. Pretty soon, we have to hush and sit down, as it's time for the business meeting. The man at the podium, standing in front of two poster-size black-and-white photographs of LBJ and JFK, begins with a prayer. "Watch over us from time to time," he implores God, before leading the group in the Pledge of Allegiance. Then, the treasurer's report: "We paid Wal-Mart for punch, $32.35, and Wal-Mart for pop, $19.60, leaving us with a balance of $6.98. Talk about cutting it close." [16]

16. In July 2006, union workers ended the nineteen-month lockout and voted to accept a contract that included an agreement to extend funding for retiree medical benefits. But by November, only 250 workers were back on the job. It was a similarly bleak year for Wal-Mart, as sales and stock fell dramatically and workers staged protests. "How much was a result of the film and the movement of Wake Up Wal-Mart, Wal-Mart Watch and the other great groups is hard to quantify," Greenwald told me. "But for sure, the fact that various studies indicate Wal-Mart has become a bad name to a significant number of socially concerned customers must be scaring the hell out of them. Hopefully, the market is telling them they have to change."

Down on the Down Low
(and Gay Marriage)

"I may be discriminated against as a homosexual if I
choose to say that about myself, but in a situation
of color, I'm discriminated against every day."

Pauline Jackson is a sixty-one-year-old church secretary at Christian Faith Fellowship Church East who worries a lot about crime and drug use and whether enough is being done to "save our children" in the black community. But if she could get our government to make any one change in this country, any change at all, it would be this: "I would make it illegal, no same-sex marriage." Which does not make me fall out of my pew at tonight's meeting of the church's women's group, called the Vessels of Honour. This is a conservative congregation, and that is how many men and women of faith feel, be they black, white, or brown.

No, it is otherwise liberal black women, both churchgoing and secular, who have startled me with the force of their feeling on this issue. My first clue came on one of my early trips, to Portland, Oregon, where a Bush-bashing counselor's assistant for a drug and alcohol program mentioned that she might peel off from the Democratic Party one day over gay marriage—once George W. is safely out of office, that is. In '04, "I thought about how, because of your gay lover being on your health insurance, my costs will go up," said the woman, Lianne Roland, who is twenty-eight. She stuck with the Democrats in that election because, when she thought about the president, "I was more scared of him than of gay marriage."

In the break room of Project Network, the treatment center in downtown Portland where Lianne works, her coworker Linda Coleman Chess, also a woman of color and a Democrat, seconded that. "What happened to the one-woman-one-man thing? Because I have a nine-year-old son, and I don't want him to see two dudes walking down the street kissing." A third black colleague, Liliane Thirdgill, said she worried that allowing gay marriage "would also change sex education in school" in a way she would not be remotely comfortable with.

As I continued my travels, I kept hearing similar comments from black women. Could the Democratic Party take a hit with them over gay marriage? I began to suspect so, but I'm not talking to vast numbers of women, and though people can tell us things polling data never can, the reverse is true, too, of course. So I broke down and called a pollster, David Bositis, senior policy analyst at the Joint Center for Political and Economic Studies in Washington, who specializes in this area. He said that while black women are still the most Democratic-voting group, they are also the most strongly opposed to gay marriage. In a major study he did right before the '04 election, nearly half of all black women— 48 percent—said they were opposed to any legal recognition for gay couples, compared to only 35 percent of white women, 40 percent of white men, and 44 percent of black men.

Bositis did not find this particularly startling; he told me I should keep in mind that because so many black men are incarcerated, the noninstitutionalized black population is 56 percent female, "which means there are *many* more black women than men" in the marriage pool. "And the other thing I suspect might contribute to it is the 'down low' phenomenon" of hidden bisexuality in the African-American community, which has made some black women see gay men as the competition.

(Oprah Winfrey opened this particular closet for a lot of people when she interviewed J. L. King, author (with Karen Hunter) of the best seller *On the Down Low: A Journey into the Lives of "Straight" Black Men Who Sleep with Men*. In his book, King speaks from his own experience when he explains how "A DL man doesn't like gay behavior. He will not be caught around anyone or anything that even looks gay. He's the first one to stand up in church and shout, 'Get the homosexuals out of here!'")

Bositis points out, too, that the fastest-growing group of people infected with the HIV virus that causes AIDS is African-American women, partly as a result of bisexual behavior, "so there are reasons to it. There are some issues there in terms of women who think they'll probably never get married and black married women who wonder about their husbands."

All of which does add up to at least a potential opening for Republicans—and one that Democrats may not find so easy to address. Tiptoeing past the issue isn't working. Yet, as I've learned, making the fairness argument to black women also seems to be a nonstarter; when Democrats call the push for gay marriage a new front in the civil rights movement, it goes over about as well among African-Americans as it would if you compared any other atrocity to the holocaust in conversation with a survivor. It's only here in Milwaukee, though, near the end of my journey, that several progressive black women break down for me just why that is.

Teresa Thomas-Boyd is a longtime community and civil rights activist and the director of Citizen Action Milwaukee, a nonpartisan public interest organization "dedicated to social, economic, and environmental justice for all." Like others I talk to here, Teresa suspects that some local black pastors were essentially bought off by President Bush, with faith-based dollars that she says give the appearance of being tied to endorsements from the pulpit. "In my heart, they used us" on the gay marriage issue, Teresa says. Still, that was possible only because "the Democratic Party has not done a good job with the faith issues. Rather than talk about it, we ignore it, so that puts people in the situation that says, 'Well, you don't even care, and somebody else is going to give us ten thousand dollars.'"

If Democrats don't mention gay marriage, she says, "and Republicans come in and make it a thorn and a sore," then guess who wins? By the time Democrats realized the issue could not be ignored in the black community, she says, "it was 'Talk to the hand,' and the conversation was over."

It starts to sound like a no-win proposition for Democrats, though, when Teresa goes on to say it's when they *do* engage on this issue that they get themselves into real trouble, by likening discrimination against gay people to racial discrimination. "In the African-American community, they see homosexuality as a chosen lifestyle, and I don't *choose* to be black," she says.

Even if sexual orientation is no more chosen than race—and research strongly indicates that is the case—Teresa says gays and lesbians can choose whether or not to disclose their sexual orientation. "I may be discriminated against as a homosexual if I choose to say that about myself, but in a situation of color, I'm discriminated against every day. The difference is so— You can't compare it. So when people want to make it the same, it's not, and it makes people angry to say that once again, we have to be the lowest of the low. Once again, another group has to have their rights, and we still don't." Clearly, Teresa is among those who feel that way.

Her parents were Baptists, but when she was growing up here in the 1960s, she and her sister sang in the choir at a Lutheran church in her neighborhood where "you had part of the congregation ready for change and some who wanted to continue to sing the German hymns. We had a pastor who was white but had marched in Alabama and wanted the change" to more contemporary music, "so he stood and said, 'I'm embracing the culture.' One Sunday, we were threatened that if we sang what we wanted to sing, the congregation would walk out, and they did." She was nine at the time, and still remembers watching over half of the people in church that morning stand up and head for the door.

The choir was invited all over "and we went south, and we did again meet up with some reality. In some cities, we'd get there and they had changed their minds about welcoming us into their homes, so you still had to do the concerts, but it was 'You can't come into our house.' One time we slept in a church, and we cried a lot and ministered to each other. The other thing that was painful was the children would say things to us, like 'We couldn't let you guys come in our house.' Our last name was Crump, and one guy in Texas who was in the church said, 'We've got some famous Crumps here in Texas, and you were probably on one of our plantations.' Those are things that stay in your head." So to mention gay rights in the same breath as civil rights, "you have to understand, in this culture they don't see it as the same, and if they don't, they don't. People weren't sensitive enough."

Teresa's friend and coworker Linda Gaskin, who pastors a small home church called the Elohim Outreach Ministries, says it was partly because she did not find Bush at all credible in his opposition to gay marriage that she had no trouble deciding to vote against him. "I'm not for same-sex marriage, because the Word of God says, 'Plentify the Earth,' and we can't change what's in the Bible. I knew it was not a sincere thing—Bush could not care less about those things—but our people were so tricked by Republicans in '04 with 'Vote your values.' Switching over is kind of like a fad."

Still another generally liberal friend of Teresa's, Patricia Parker, who pastors the Craig Memorial CME Church, says she "broke camp" with the Democrats a long time ago, not over gay marriage but because "they have taken African-Americans for granted." She considers herself an independent voter now and says, "I think it's time for a third party."

She feels that "there are some issues on gay folks," but "there are a lot of gay folks in the church," too. "Is it biology or is it a choice?" Either way, "they're still our children; we don't hate the sinner." Pat is potting some impatiens out in back of her apartment, along with a friend who is staying with her. In most ways, she says, she is still in sync with the Democrats' agenda, but on the culture issues, no. "If you don't like the Ten Commandments in a public place, then don't look at it. That's what this country was based on." As she says this, a car tears through the alley behind her house, tires squealing and music blasting, and she calls out, "You know *she* doesn't live here."

Her friend Lauren Brown-Perry, an attorney, thinks voting Republican has become almost a status symbol for younger black women in particular, and "everyone wants to have it."

Though still a Democrat herself, Lauren has no illusions: "My mother had a patronage job in Chicago, so she was a building captain in the projects" for the Democratic Party, "and 'vote early and often' was serious. We knew elections were coming because they'd clean up the neighborhood, and milk and mail would get delivered, and they'd give out T-shirts with the number of the lever you had to pull. Then, after the election, it would go back to normal." Lauren is pretty sure her daughter, a student at Tennessee State University, is a flat-out Republican at this point. "She's conservative," Lauren says, no question. "We always taught her 'Vote the person, not the party,' and when she voted in '04, she said, 'That's private.'" So many black women she knows have become Republicans, Pat says, "that we've got a lot of closet Democrats. They like the freedom of choice, as quiet as it's kept."

Pat is convinced that, like the Democratic voters who were bought off with T-shirts under the old Chicago machine, the churches that got faith-based funds and then preached for Bush "got bought out," she says, then claps her hand over her mouth, as if she hadn't meant to let that slip. The Republicans, she says, "came with money in their hands." Of course, absent a thank-you note—"'We so enjoyed the payola, and hope that if we keep milking that gay marriage thing, there will be more where that came from'"—that sort of link is impossible to prove.

The Christian Faith Fellowship Church—the parent church of the one where I'm attending an evening meeting of the Vessels of Honour—is among those that received faith-based funds, about $1 million over three years for a program to encourage physical activity among young people. Yet though all of the fourteen women at the meeting say they did vote for Bush in '04, when I listen to them, I don't see them as marching in political lockstep, and I do hear criticism of the president. And even among these intensely traditional believers, I see plenty of openings for Democrats.

They are not what you'd call wary of a stranger; one woman in the group opens her arms and yells, "Give me some love," when I walk in. Their female copastor, Evon Green, leads them in a political discussion that she says fits right in with the group's overall "character-building" theme. It was the trauma of having an abortion herself when she was a young woman that led her into the ministry, Evon says, so that's what she preaches on, teaches on, and votes on. Yet despite the apparent unanimity of opinion here on abortion and gay marriage, these women also voice considerable dissatisfaction with their government on the bread-and-butter issues—housing, education, and perhaps most of all, Medicare and health care for seniors.

At one point, Evon tosses out a hypothetical: "The president is in and out of Milwaukee all the time, and if you ran into him and he came up to give you that handshake and said, 'What can I do for you?' It's your once-in-a-lifetime opportunity. So what do you say?"

The first response she gets, from a church member named Peggy Neal, is "'Hey, dude, turn from your wicked ways.' He's playing the fence, claiming to be a Christian. . . . It's 'Vote for me; I'll set you free,' and the band plays on. It's almost like he's selling us out under the table."

Later in the discussion, Peggy elaborates, "I would invite him and have a deliverance service for him and take him into the inner city, and then I would ask him, 'Now what do you think?'" Which, as I'm walking away after the final gospel song, makes me think that while the gay marriage issue is undeniably a problematic one for Democrats, Republicans hoping to make serious inroads with black women still have a long, long way to go.

Between the Rivers

*"If Al Gore ran, now I'd be willing to listen
to him, and that is a big deal for me to say that."*

I t's just the three of us, Cathy and Pam and me, out on the back swing at Cath's house on Kentucky Lake—us and the lightning bugs. My kids are upstairs asleep, finally, and we have been putting off talking politics to the point that we have exhausted even such topics as the pros and cons of a Brazilian wax, and that those little Tide pen spot removers that Kelly Ripa pitches work pretty well, actually. I don't know if there really are whole worlds of subjects I would never cover with anyone else, but there are definitely places I only go with them.

When I ask what's going on around Mount Carmel, where we all grew up, Pam says that with the price of a barrel of oil up so high, they are drilling around there again and even reopening some of the old wells. But, while a few people are doing better, most are not, and Cath reports that the local paper, the *Daily Republican Register*, is really struggling to stay afloat because "there are so few businesses left in Mount Carmel that they don't have the ads." There is such little traffic on Market Street that some of the stoplights blink red all the time now, so you no longer have to sit through a light when there's no one else on the block. There is a new doctor in town who can set a broken bone, but still no pediatrician, so a lot of kids get their medical care in the ER. Crystal meth has become such a big problem that there have been two busts right on Pam's well-tended block on Chestnut Street. And it's for her public health job that she's just finished the (partly made-up) James Frey book *A Million Little Pieces,* about his addiction and rehab.

The capper di tutti cappers, though, comes when Cath tells about how a bunch of graduating high school seniors in Princeton, Indiana, where she lives, just across the river from Mount Carmel, got in trouble for having one of the "naked parties that are the big thing now." Of course, I live outside staid old fully-clothed Washington, so I am not hip to this latest adaptive strategy on the global warming front.

Sure, she says, and the even bigger thing is groups of kids driving around naked; a carload of teenagers in Fairfield, Illinois, where Kim lives, was hauled into the police station like that, and one parent, "smart mom, when she went to pick her boy up, she didn't bring him anything to put on. She said, 'I thought no clothes were no problem.'" (By phone, Kim confirms the case of the naked cruisers. "That actually did happen," she says when she stops laughing.) Still, I have a hard time squaring the idea of these bacchanalia with my impression that kids in Mount Carmel these days might be even churchier than we were; a group called Aces for Christ—featured prominently on the website of the public high school we attended—meets every Friday morning in the school library. Then again, they could be praying for naked parties for all I know.

I have given my friends due warning that I am here to talk to them for this project, and to reinterview some of the other women I heard from on my first foray, to see if anything in the past eighteen months has changed their political views and made them any more or less likely to go with the Republicans in '08. We have decided that to do the conversation justice, we need to take a couple of days at Cathy's place, floating in the water off her dock. But because we don't agree, we are leaving in the morning and still haven't gotten around to this planned political discussion. So, it's time.

Pam and Cathy both exhale before we dive in, and I see another reason we haven't gone there sooner; Pam is still a Democrat and Cathy still a Republican, but we all agree that the outlook is depressing. "I'm more worried than I was" even in February of '05, Pam says, and Cathy is right behind her: "Yeah, because of the war."

"I'm concerned about my financial security, and I'm very concerned about the environment," Pam goes on. "If my children decided not to have children, I'm okay with it. That's how concerned I am. The billionaires just got a tax cut, and they won't raise the minimum wage, and there's no hope of women getting to stay home with their children." Again, Cath is right there with her: "And more and more people are uninsured." In Illinois, Pam says, "you've got All Kids"—which in theory provides coverage for children in low-income families—"but the practitioners won't take it." That's partly because the state is so behind in its payments to those providers who will accept Medicaid. "Health care and gas and college costs have all increased, but have incomes increased? No."

Pam's own situation is somewhat better than it was eighteen months ago because her husband, Stan, has a business-side job for the coal company now; he's out of the mine and "*so* much happier. He works a lot of hours, but he gets to use his education." But with their daughter Chloe—who withdrew her application to West Point in the end—heading off to Hanover College in Indiana in the fall, they've got some major expenses coming up, even with the partial academic scholarship she earned, and Pam is thinking she might have to quit the public health job she loves and take something better-paid in a hospital.

Cathy is still nursing elderly patients, through a home health agency, and says Medicare is more messed up than ever. "Let's say we have a patient with an open wound. Before, you could go every day and get paid. But now you get a lump sum no matter how many times you go, so the kind of care that patient is going to get all depends on your ethics. People who are blind and can't give themselves their insulin twice a day, *no* health agency wants to take that patient anymore—and now we have to teach people who are not capable how to do the care for people who were really too sick to leave the hospital in the first place. So I don't like the medical part" of what this Republican administration and Congress have come up with, "but yet, on the business side, when Mike and I talk about it . . ." She doesn't finish the sentence.

Has she found that in her family's experience, the Republicans have been good for business? She's not positive about that, from what she hears from her husband, a partner in her brother's construction company: "Mike says they're bidding now what it costs just to keep everybody working, and they did twice as much last year and still made less money." But she is not considering switching her vote, because "if we had a Democrat in there, would it be better?"

This seems to be more than Pam can bear, since she hardly sees how it could be any worse. "I think George Bush is corrupt. I think he's evil. And they go around talking about God all the time? You talk it, but you don't walk it, buddy." Which is shocking only because this is Pam talking, Pam who I don't think had a bad word for anyone in all four years of *high school*.

"I'm not in love with Bush, but it's the business side" that wins out with her, Cathy says. While Pam doesn't see that any but the very wealthiest have benefited, even on the business side: "I feel like we're a country put together with toothpicks, and I have a feeling of insecurity" about the economy. "Do you ever go to the grocery store and see all the people who pay with their credit card? A lady I saw the other day was buying diapers with her credit card." Not as a matter of convenience, either, but because she had to.

I have to give Cathy a lot of credit for hanging in there with this discussion; she is not getting mad, and she is not changing her mind. "I'm not saying the Republicans are great, because I don't think they're any better," she says evenly. "I think they all lie."

"And that's why people don't vote," Pam says. But Cathy suggests that might be why people *do* vote, or rather, why they vote the way they do. "The ads just try to mix you up. Who is telling the truth?" If you're not sure and you find both sides more or less equally untrustworthy, "just best serve the need *you* have; just go serve yourself." And though I am so over all the media bashing from left, right, and center, especially now that the First Amendment itself is so clearly under assault, there is no avoiding the fact that our journalistic compulsion that there be a tit for every single tat has made it all too easy to conclude, as Cathy has, that there is no way to know who's telling the truth about anything. "Both of them lie," she says again of the two parties, "so without vast knowledge, I'll stay with what's comfortable."

Then she circles back to something we'd been talking about before. My mom is from Kentucky, and her people are from around here—right around here, as in out there under the water somewhere, in fact. Our family was pushed off their farmland in the Cumberland River bottoms between the Cumberland and Tennessee rivers back when they built Kentucky Dam during World War II, creating what's now Kentucky Lake. They were forced out a second time, from where they'd moved out on Jenny Ridge, not far away, when they were flooding the Cumberland to form Lake Barkley in the 1960s. And they had barely settled into their new home just a few miles down the road, in Golden Pond, when the Tennessee Valley Authority (TVA) knocked a third time, to announce that they would need that land—the whole town, as it turned out—for the Land Between the Lakes recreation area, where they've since installed attractions like the "elk and bison prairie" I had no interest in as a kid, and the planetarium my kids don't want to go to now. If you take a little two-lane highway called the Trace from what used to be Jenny Ridge past what used to be Golden Pond, you can visit Homestead 1850, "a living, working historical farm" that "features real people working on the farm, doing various activities."

My great-grandmother, Mama Bleidt, the woman my daughter Della Lane was named for, said she believed she'd rather die than be put out of her home a third time, and that's what she did. So when we stopped by the Land Between the Lakes visitors' center earlier, and read their narrative about the history of the place, I told my friends I had to admit I'd never even heard the other side of the story growing up—the part about how great all of this development was. "So it's kind of like your family and the TVA," Cathy says now. "You feel like you never have the whole story." So, instead of being manipulated, go with the sure thing: self-interest.

This is an appealingly straightforward formulation, I have to say, and one that would seem to involve a minimum of self-deception. But it's not so much that we don't ever have all the facts as that very often, we do not even want them; I am just not that interested in the "whole story" of all that the TVA accomplished in Appalachia, for example, any more than Cathy wants to hear a lot more on the unhappy subject of Mr. Bush's decisions and their consequences. Yet even without what she calls vast knowledge, I am positive that there was a way to create electrical power and jobs in western Kentucky without moving those families over and over and all but stealing their land outright. Just like it's clear that we can do what's "good for business," in the end creating even more jobs in clean technology, and still do right by the environment.

Either to believe everything that we are told—*The New York*

Times hates America!—or to throw up our hands and say, "Who can know?" is to abdicate our responsibility as shareholders in our democracy. Yet non sequitur as a lifestyle is catching on: If you question our involvement in Iraq, then you are in league with al Qaeda! And as a worldview, a carefully constructed view of the world as we have decided to see it, based on the information we have decided to take in, this is not entirely irrational. On the contrary, it is strategic, not only for those in power but also for those who prefer to think of themselves as powerless. In general, as Cathy herself suggests, I'd say most of us know just about exactly as much as we want to know, and then act accordingly.

On our way to the lake, I stopped off in Evansville to have lunch with our classmate Carol Woodard, who works as a cardio rehab nurse. Women always say, "You look the same!" but for the record, Carol really does. She feels the same, too, about her vote for Bush in '04, and about the condescension of the Democrats. She lived in L.A. for some years before moving back to this area to be near her father before he died. "That was a big transition, from Jaguars to pickup trucks," she says. She has been drifting to the right in the years since, and voted for Bush last time "because I feel a little bit looked down on as a Christian in my own family"— by the Democrats in her own family, she means.

Why is it as a Christian that she feels looked down on by Democrats, though? "To me, Republicans are in a box that we're all Christian, idiots and stupid. I think that's something I've been feeling for years and that even affects my spiritual walk; I don't want to judge anybody, but I don't want to be in that box. When they put Bush down, I take it personally as a Christian. I feel they are putting down something about his spirituality, and that makes me angry at the Democrats, and that's terrible," because "then I'm shut down and don't want to discuss it." At which point, "I don't have the time or the desire to be more educated." Respect is a prerequisite, then, for the willingness to work at acquiring that vast knowledge Cathy was talking about. Without that respect, without feeling recognized and taken seriously, it only stands to reason that, as Carol says, "I'm shut down and I don't want to discuss it."

Back in Mount Carmel, at the Wabash County Health Department, Pam's coworkers have been swayed by events over the last eighteen months, though they seem loath to admit it—maybe because we call the ability to respond to new information "flip-flopping," now, which sounds even worse than when it was "a woman's prerogative." Pam's boss, Patti Skees, who was so unhappy with the president when we talked before, says she's just trying to get through these last two Bush years as calmly as possible. One of her sons recently joined the navy, "and you really have to watch it on the website for navy moms, because people think you're against the troops" if you criticize the government in any way. "So I've backed off a little bit for my own peace of mind; now I just watch the birds and the squirrels out the window and try to let it all go."

Patti would seem to have more company these days as she's taking those deep breaths, because even in this county—which, again, is nearly evenly split between Republicans and Democrats but went 70 percent for Bush in '04—Democrats who had drifted away are at least talking like they're on their way home. Patti surprises me, though, when she says she doesn't think of herself that way—as a Democrat, that is. Though intensely critical of the Bush administration, "I'm not liberal. I'm not pro-choice." She has in no way softened toward what she sees as the intransigence and extremism of the current administration: "They're talking gay rights and flag burning, and it's all a diversion. It's our servicemen who are paying the price. Even these young men who are up for murder; it's so confused over there they don't know who the enemy is, so those kids are the scapegoats. They don't listen to anyone with expertise." But this passionate opposition has not made her into a Democrat because both parties, she says, offend her with intellectually dishonest claims. With Patti, the hard sell has backfired to the point that "I don't trust anybody" in the political arena. "And they may say we're all either right-wing Republicans or left-wing Democrats, but I don't think that's true. I think we want out of Iraq, to continue the war on terror, if that's what it is, and we need some protection for the middle class and some accountability in government." Who says the middle is muddled?

What Patti says about wanting to get out of Iraq *and* to wage a real war on terror could hardly be more to the point. I don't have any reason to believe the Democrats lost the last presidential election over the terror issue, and I fail to see why it would be a political problem for the party going forward; our sixteen intelligence agencies finally agree on something, and it's that operations in Iraq have been one long recruitment ad for the terrorists. A majority of the Iraqis we went in to liberate and protect now say they approve of attacks on American troops. Homeland security is such that a man recently walked through an unguarded door in the U.S. Capitol with a loaded gun and ran from floor to floor—in a building where we've spent $2 billion on security since 9/11—until a civilian finally intervened, lifted the intruder off his feet, and handed him to the cops.

Yet for other than political reasons, the Democrats need to listen closely to the one security mom I did find, a woman I already knew in Washington, who voted for Bush in '04 but didn't tell anybody, she said, because so many of her friends are not only Democrats but worked for Kerry. "I *despised* George Bush. I'm one of the few people who liked Gore more and more as the campaign went on, and I couldn't stand Bush's mannerisms; his whole life story pissed me off and still does. But then 9/11 happened. Where was he? I saw him hiding behind Karen Hughes's skirt, but we also had this very real enemy, and I started to see events in a different way. I started to see there's no appeasing this; you wipe it out as a political philosophy, and that's going to be a bloody thing. A couple of months after 9/11, we went to New York, and my sister-in-law is this ardent New Yorker—there were still smoldering holes in the ground!—and we said something about the nature of this enemy, and she said, 'There are reasons why it happened.' I said, 'What do you mean?' and she said, 'Well, our policies.' And it was this almost cinematic moment where I looked across the room and saw this stack of *The Nation* and saw that we were going one way and the people we used to agree with were going the other. For me to actually vote for Bush is shocking—shocking." But that's what she did.

I personally have never heard any Democrat make as cavalier a statement about the war on terror as our president did when he said he didn't give Osama bin Laden all that much thought, so I do not share my friend's provisional trust in the guy behind Karen's skirt. Yet she is right about the urgency of the threat, and deserves to know that the party she'd rather vote for takes it every bit as seriously as she does.

This summer, on a long car trip out west, our family listened to the audio version of Taylor Branch's book *At Canaan's Edge: America in the King Years 1965–68*. We got to hear, and not just read, the words he quotes from Lyndon Johnson about how American voters will "forgive you for anything except being weak." That's why Johnson stayed in a war he'd feared from the start could not be won. But he was not at all wrong about how Americans respond to weakness—from Michael Dukakis's failure to rhetorically rip a nonexistent rapist's head off, to John Kerry's interminable hesitation before taking a swing at the Swifties who'd questioned his war record.

Much of the criticism I've heard of Democrats over the last eighteen months boils down to a suspicion of inner weakness. The only antidote is the kind of courage we see again and again in Branch's history of the faith-based, unashamedly idealistic, outlandishly overmatched civil rights movement. Even from the distance of a few decades, it's easy to fool ourselves into thinking that the change King and others brought about was inevitable, somehow, when what they really did was the impossible. And because it's not only Americans but our enemies who will, as LBJ said, forgive anything except weakness, Democrats don't just need to project strength, they need to be strong.

When I talked to Pam's coworker Candy Kemper at the Health Department in early '05, she described herself as a Democrat who had gone for Bush twice because she couldn't bear the alternatives. Now, looking toward '08, what she says is, "The funny thing is, if Gore ended up running, I might— He has a different perspective on things now, after all he's been through, and I think he'd be a strong candidate. Before, I just didn't think he was strong. Now you listen to Gore, and you can tell he's a stronger person than he was before, and that he has some insight into things." She doesn't see weakness in his loss, but strength in how he came through it. Her coworker Rita Miller says she is definitely back with the Democrats. "Last time it was just because I didn't like the other guy; what was his name?" Their supervisor, Cindy Strickland Brown, who describes herself as "more anti-Bush than ever," says her pick might be Edwards in '08. "It should have been Edwards-Kerry" last time, she thinks. "There's nothing obnoxious about him." A slogan at last.

A newspaper colleague of mine used to talk about how important it was for her as a writer to know for whom she was writing. Not only who her reader was, but for whom, when she was typing away, the whole effort was really intended. And in that sense, my project has from the start been for Kim as much as for anyone, with me still on that hiking trail in West Virginia trying to win her over, and wondering what it would take. She couldn't get away to come to Kentucky with us, so I drive over to Fairfield to see her one afternoon. I'm kind of beside myself when, over a cup of coffee with a couple of the high school teachers I talked to the last time I was here, she casually drops this: "You know who I'm liking better than I used to? Al Gore. He's gotten more human; the guy I see now, I would have been more prone to vote for."

Is she kidding? Is this a sign of the Apocalypse? No, no, and she is all nonchalance: "I saw him on some talk show and on *Saturday Night Live,* and he was hilarious. If Al Gore ran, now I'd be willing to listen to him, and that is a big deal for me to say that."

"I would, too," says her friend Lori Robson, who is a pretty committed Republican. The worst time to size up a politician is when he's actually running for something, says Lori's fellow teacher Pam Robbins: "It's like right before they pick the homecoming queen, the girls are nicer: 'Hi, I came to watch your volleyball game!'"

None of which means Kim wants to hear a negative word about the current occupant of the Oval Office. "There's been so much more loss over there than I ever thought there would be," she says of Iraq. "But I don't think there's a point to making statements like that; what good does it do? I don't have a problem with him." Pam says that her son-in-law has served in the war, and her daughter "says that whenever he gets back from the desert, they have to be very careful about loud noises. He's very much a supporter, but then, when you're military, you'd better be saying that."

"And talk about being programmed," Kim says. "They are programmed to say that." You look like my friend Kim Hungerford, but you are not, are you? *What have you done with her?*

Lori feels that it was still important to remove Saddam Hussein. "If no one stands up, it's Hitler again." But Kim's double seems to think there must be more to the story than late-breaking qualms about long-running repression in Iraq. "There's always a benefit to us, and not just because we're a wonderful nation," that we march off to war. "There are so many suffering countries. . . . I just support the military, and the decision has been made, so I don't want to say anything negative."

When we inevitably get around to abortion, Pam, who is pro-choice, and Kim, who is pro-life, parry a little, and not for the first time. "We've talked and talked about this, and I just couldn't tell someone they couldn't" have an abortion, Pam says.

"And I could," says Kim.

"And I have a poster that says, 'Respect is agreeing to disagree,'" Lori puts in.

It's because we've lost sight of that respect that our political system is so broken, Kim says, and again brings up Al Gore. It's because she feels a new respect *from* him as much as for him—and senses humility instead of condescension—that she feels first-name friendly toward him now. "I'd listen to Al, and be able to overlook the robot stuff, because now I know he's actually human." Pam is not ready to go that far: "He's been 'the son of,' and he thinks he's entitled." Well, Kim says, "he may have changed his attitude now. Humble pie really does make a difference." Interestingly, humility does not look like weakness to her, but just the opposite.

Afterward, in the car, I have to say I'm in awe of her open mind; at this point, George Bush could come up with a cure for AIDS while rebuilding NOLA's Lower Ninth with his own hands, and I'd still squint and think hard thoughts—though I do always try to hold in mind the image of him as a little boy, waiting for his parents to bring his younger sister home from the hospital in New York, because no one had told him that she'd died of leukemia, so when they arrived, he was looking for her and asking where she was.

There is a line in a favorite book of mine, Shirley Hazzard's *The Transit of Venus,* about the hero's admirable willingness to revise an unfavorable first impression: "As to the hired couple at Peverel, the Mullions, Ted Tice learned afterwards that they had lost their grandson in an accident some weeks before. If you knew enough, antipathy would rarely be conclusive." Knowing enough to get past both apathy *and* antipathy takes work, but vitriol is no less the enemy than passivity, I think, because it makes us crazy, and crazy is not working.

Now, I know plenty of smart politics guys who would argue that vitriol works pretty well, actually, and that whoever has the harshest and most extreme campaign message—and thus, the most pumped-up base—wins. I would counter that Democrats are often so profoundly and even proudly unskilled in this area—case in point: John Kerry trying to spit out the nonsecret that Dick Cheney's daughter is a 1-1-lesbian and clearly not feeling good about it—that doing the decent thing can also be the smart thing.

It's so telling that when Al Gore won Kim over—Kim, who once said that even if we were poisoning the earth, "maybe that's how this planet is supposed to end"—it was not with lectures and proofs but with humanity, with "humble pie." You might not guess that a vulnerability deficit would be a problem for the Democrats at this point. But as I look back over all of my interviews, one of the things that comes through most consistently is the desire for much more of that.

Paradoxically, we want both more strength and more humility, and they are not at all mutually exclusive. The perception that Bush had both qualities in more or less equal measure was probably the key to his appeal. He seemed strong in himself and yet also came across as Everyman and then some, with the critical ability to laugh at himself. Until the public wearied of him for other reasons, people kind of liked it when Bush forgot himself and slapped his wife's backside or bumped his head getting on the plane or tried to bolt through a locked door. "I know that guy," they said, "and he's okay." Whereas if I had even the tiniest sliver of my Kentucky grandmother's buttermilk pie for every time someone had brought up Kerry's windsurfing over the last eighteen months, I would be a big, big girl by now. "I do *not* know that guy," they said. Maybe in Nantucket or on the Vineyard, it gave folks that frisson of recognition, but elsewhere, he might as well have taken to wearing an ascot or enlivening campaign events by singing "Ne Me Quitte Pas" to his wife. You can't win on issues alone, even if they are on your side.

As it turns out, what women want from the Democrats is just this: everything. But we'd settle for respect, a willing ear, and a comfort level with the faith that is a big part of life for a lot of us. Maybe more than anything, we want to be heard, and ultimately, of course, it is up to us to make sure that we are. In the hope that somebody is listening, I'm going to give the last word to Kim: "You can listen and listen to these guys, all the speeches and all the debates. But if you're not sure you believe what they're saying, or you think they're just saying what you want to hear, that makes it difficult. And the person—the man or woman—who could break through that, that person truly would have it made."

Acknowledgments

My warmest thanks to all of the women who shared their thoughts and their time with me over the last eighteen months; you made this journey the greatest pleasure of my professional life. I set out to hear from women of all ages, races, regions, tax brackets, and points of view, and found that astonishing generosity and openness cut across all of the above.

Anyone who thinks we are so polarized that we have lost all ability to talk to one another only has to listen to these women to think again: Emily Abrams, Luz Aguilar, Lisa Alexander, Rachel Arndt, Lois Arnold, Bridgette Aronson, Mary Jane Arrington, Kristen Aston, Barbara Bachus, Charline Baird, Beth Barach, Charlene Barnard, Amanda Barrick, Sara Bechtold, Paula Beehn, Minnie Bellamy, Blanche Benson, Mandy Berg, Ferowni Beshir, Laveda Bhachu, Lucy Billiter, Betty Blatt, Betty Bowers, Angella Bowman, Teresa Thomas-Boyd, Cindy Brown, Denita Brown, Susan Buck, Robin Burrow, Jeanine Cahill, Christina Carmody, Lynn Chachere, K. K. Chambers, Polly Chaplin, Sandy Chico, Betty Clarke, Linda Coleman Chess, Amy Cohen, Jeanne Condol, Virginia Connally, Carol Cordell, Missy Corrigan, Cindy Crumley,

ACKNOWLEDGMENTS

Diana Crump, Elizabeth Cruz, Ann Curtis, Gloria Dauphin, Liz Davis, Elizabeth De Angelo, Georgene Delso, Joan Domico, Erika Donnellson, Kelly Dore, Kitty Dukakis, Mary Earl, Jeannie Economos, Julie Ellis, Ceci Estelle, Cynthia Farin, Nicole Fedder, Ashley Fishburn, Linda Gaskin, Doreen Geiger, Nancy Gilgannon, Jackie Gilliland, Libby Gray, Evon Green, Margie Green, Becky Haigler, Jewel Halford, Yvonne Hardy, Kirtley Harris, Terry Haskett, Jill Hastings, Joyce Haught, Linda Herrera, Pam Hertlein, Stephanie Higgins, Margaret Hoffman, Nancy Horton, Judy Howard, Dorothy Hudoch, Kathleen Huff, Anne Humes, Kim Hungerford, Mary Hurd, Pauline Jackson, Robin Jackson, Pam Kaiser, Candy Kemper, Cindy Kent, Denise Kent, Viola Kieffer, Carolyn Kildebrand, Loretta Kinney, Pegg Knechtges, Helen Kottemann, Cheryl Kush, Cheryl Lanch, Martha Leasure, Wendy Lee, Gail Lemarie, Kim Licht, Jenna Lihvarcik, Victoria Lopez, Martha Lynch, Susan Lynch, Maria Luna, Ruth Ann Madera; C.A., Suann Maier, Dora Martinez, Mitzi Mattox, Ann May, Sheila Mayhorn, Maureen McCormack, Meagan McCrackin, Angela McDonald, Kathleen McDonald, Sheryl McGee, Nancy McKinnis, Sara McNelis, Michele Mendoza, Peggy Merical, Beth Mewhinney, Sharon Meyer; M.D., Nadia Meza, Noel Miles, Jesse Miller, Lavaunne Miller, Rita Miller, Anne Milling, Keri Mitchell, Renée Mitchell, Mary Monnat, Joyce Moore, Freya Motafram, Judy Mullinnax, Mary Musgrave, Mary Ann Nash, Peggy Neal, Pat Orr, Patricia Parker, Jighnesa Patel, Sejal Patel, Jody Perry, Lauren Brown-Perry, Janie Poe, Thalia Potter, Cathy Raber, Barbara Ann Radnofsky, Vickie Raines, Emily Ray, Lillie Rees, Donna Reever, Sharleyn Regino, Joanne Reinhardt, Julia Rientjes, Lori Robson, Jill Rock, Lianne Roland, Cheryl Rossiter, Jean Ryan, Nanette Schoenewe, Magdalena Schwartz, Meenakshi Shelat, Alena Simcox, Joan Skees, Patti Skees, Christina Skillman, Pam Smittle, Carol Anne Socash, Jamila Spencer, Alice Spier, Peggy Spier, Susie Stockard, Ellen Sweet, Carmen Talemente, Liz Tarone,

ACKNOWLEDGMENTS

Sharon Tenbarge, Hakimah Terry, Suzanne Thibault; C.A., Liliane Thirdgill, Sherry Throop, Emily Timmons, Frankie Tobin, Marlene Turnbach, Meghan Umlauf, Shirley Underwood, Angela Vasquez, Anna Vedro, Terry Veets, Mary Verra, Cristina Vicente, Dorothy Voege, Jill Vrabel, Kathy Welch, Stephanie Westman, Pam Whetstone, Katie White, Shirley Wick, Sue Johnson Wilkinson, Karen Willenbring; C.A.; M.D., Shelley Willet, Regina Winter, Kristen Wolff, Carol Woodard, Pam Wonnell, Becky Zaheri, and JoAnn Zartman.

Several people have asked how I went about finding these women. I decided the where first, then lined up several interviews in that place, quite at random—either through friends of friends, a local organization of some kind, or maybe a mention in a news account. Almost no one said no, and most everyone I met then turned me over to her friends, and so on. Most of the time, I had no idea where these women would line up politically until they told me themselves.

There would have been no book—ever, I think—without a nudge from the amazing Gail Ross, agent and ace human being. Or without my editor, Alice Mayhew, who believed in my meanderings from the start, and her wonderful right hand at Simon & Schuster, Serena Jones.

The inspiration for this project came from a weekend getaway with my blood sister since fifth grade, Pam Wonnell, and our adopted sibs of thirty-plus years, Cathy Raber and Kim Hungerford, and from an e-mail exchange with Emily "Prudie" Yoffe. I would still be mulling the intro if not for the Thursday-morning C & O Canal walks with my smart neighbor Michelle Brafman.

I'm so thankful to all of the friends who so kindly shared their friends—and their couches, moral support, and more—while I was on the road, especially Mary Monnat and Steve Slater, Ed and Cindy Timms, Colleen O'Connor, Paula and Edward Hughes, Cliff and Pam Foster, Robert Tobin, and John Chaplin.

ACKNOWLEDGMENTS

Thanks also to Mount Carmel content specialist James Daniel Daubs and to my fixers Beth Barach, Judy Benjamin, Lori Bernat, Polly Chaplin, Maggie Clarke, Elizabeth De Angelo, Terry Haskett, Susan Kottemann, Ana Maria Mendez, Mary Ann Nash, Janie Poe, Mauro and Carol Pondo, Magdalena Schwartz, Jon and Lisa Stanger, Frankie Tobin, and Marlene Turnbach.

Several known *streghe*—Laura Lippman, Catherine Manegold, and Michelle Brafman—did me the enormous favor of reading the manuscript with care and a critical eye. Anne Noble and Dale Loy either never tired of hearing about these women or have missed their calling, Peter Kaufman made a couple of important suggestions, and Carl Wagner offered crucial support in the home stretch. Others pitched in by coming up with possible titles, including my daughter Della, who lobbied hard for *Crossover Moms* after it occurred to her at the ice rink. And I only wish I could have taken my husband's suggestion: *Tuesdays with da Vinci*.

Behind every mom's finished project is reliable child care and I want to acknowledge the vital contribution of my patient and kindhearted babysitters, Lauren Chmielecki, Hannah Duffy, Meg Palisoul, and Elizabeth Clay.

I will always be grateful to the University of Notre Dame's Elizabeth Christman, my writing teacher and friend, whose rigor, sense of occasion, delight in "the most enduring of all life's pleasures," and habit of beginning each semester in a new ensemble, sometimes including a hat, made her my role model even before she was teaching Trollope in her eighties.

I am mindful still of my debt to Donnis Baggett, the first editor who encouraged me to have fun in print, on the state desk of *The Dallas Morning News*—and to my generous and talented former colleagues there, especially Ed Timms, receptacle of all secrets and many obscure facts.

Thanks, too, to all of the word (and idea) mavens who have schooled me and been so good to me over the years, in particular

ACKNOWLEDGMENTS

Jan Battaile and Michael Oreskes at *The New York Times,* Bill Beaman at *Reader's Digest,* Tom Watson and Mark Whitaker at *Newsweek*, and Ann McDaniel of the Washington Post Company. Thanks also to the ridiculously talented Dana Gluckstein, who made the photo session so painless.

I would fear a thunderbolt if I did not include a word of thanks to everyone who took care of me when I was recovering from cancer, especially Mary Monnat, my coconspirator since our first night in Lewis Hall, Anne and Norma Jean Noble, Lisa Pope Girion, Andra Armstrong, Gail Edmondson, and all the power pray-ers who went to work for me, including Susan, Chris, Claire, Peter and John Muller, Rose Sterr, Susan Gibbs, Elizabeth Lev, Sister Sheila Brosnan, Lynn Joyce Hunter, Pat Orr, Kay Tarrant and Betty Kilday (aka the Rosary Queens), Jorge and Vivian Peirats, and Sophie de Ravinel.

Also to the late greats, especially my grandmother, Jettie Bleidt Lawrence, who impressed on me how few things cannot be improved with a little bacon grease, and Johnny Apple, who noticed more walking by than most of us ever see.

Deepest thanks to my staunchly Republican parents, John and Freida Henneberger, whose commitments, political and otherwise, I can only admire, and to my sister and brother-in-law, Joane Henneberger and Wiley Pickett, whose hospitality is the best. Most of all, I thank my husband, the bravest man I know, and our children, Della and Connor, who at least once every day make me thank God.

Index

INDEX

INDEX

About the Author

Melinda Henneberger is a regular contributor to *Slate*, the on-line magazine, and a columnist for *Commonweal*, the Catholic opinion journal. She is a former *New York Times* reporter and a former contributing editor for *Newsweek* magazine. She lives with her husband and their two children outside Washington, D.C.